# Ghosts of You

# Ghosts of You

## The Murdered Ladies Series

By Cathy Ulrich

Okay Donkey Press

Published by Okay Donkey Press

Los Angeles, CA 90034

www.okaydonkeymag.com

First edition. October 2019

ISBN: 978-1-7332441-0-7

Library of Congress Control Number: 2019945367

Cover art: Sarah E. Shields

*This is for Miranda, and Marilyn, and Jean, and Laura, and Bonnie, and Elizabeth, and Savanna, and all the lost women.*

# TABLE OF CONTENTS

# Being the Murdered Girl

The thing about being the murdered girl is you set the plot in motion.

Your boyfriend and your best friend are going to fall in love. Your parents' marriage is going to fall apart. The neighbors will watch it happen, at awkward back-yard barbecues. Their own daughters haven't been murdered, but they'll all compare themselves to you.

You'll be a saint. You'll be a whore. You'll be the murdered girl, the first any of them have known, except the detective with a dark past who will investigate your murder. He's known tons of murdered girls. He's had his fill of them. You're nothing special to him. Except maybe you remind him of his own daughter. It's the way you're smiling in the photograph your parents give him. They'll argue over which photo to use.

The detective can tell their marriage is falling apart. It happens to the parents of murdered girls.

They'll put your picture in the entry at your school, where your classmates can go past and feel the weight of your murder. It's very heavy. Your classmates will slouch and say it's because their textbooks are too thick. They'll complain about the endless assignments on loss. Even the math teacher will focus only on subtraction for a week after your murder.

Your best friend will cry during literature class. Your boyfriend will see her crying and realize that she's beautiful. Your best friend and your boyfriend will kiss, for the first time, behind the school, waiting for the bus to come. They'll be the prom king and queen. They'll say she'd have wanted us to be happy. They'll come together while your parents are coming apart.

Your mother will wash dishes and cry and your father will retreat into silence. If your mother speaks to him, he'll only reply in grunts. The neighbors will bring casseroles. The neighbors will want for things to get back to normal. The neighbors will feel guilty about their own daughters parading around with bare shoulders and short skirts, and lock them in their bedrooms.

The neighbors' daughters will communicate with each other through a complicated series of smoke signals. One of them will have found the pack of cigarettes you used to hide down the street from the bus stop, in Mrs. Barneyback's bushes, and they'll each take cigarettes from the pack to send each other messages from their windows. The neighborhood will be filled with smoke for days.

*Looks like rain*, the adults will remark. *Looks like rain.*

## Being the Murdered Wife

The thing about being the murdered wife is you set the plot in motion.

Your husband will become a great man. Thousands of scholars will know your name. He'll say: *I couldn't have done it without her. I'd never be the man I am today without her.*

Your children will be sent to live with your husband's parents. A great man like your husband couldn't be expected to spend his time tending to his murdered wife's children. Your children will be shown photographs of you, told: *This is Mommy.* Your children will grow up thinking of mothers as two-dimensional things, will think of you as that girl with one hand holding her hair back, squinting into the camera — that photo you'd always asked your husband to throw out. That photo you never knew he kept. Your children will grow, someday, older than you.

While your children are growing up, your husband will become a great man. He will write poems in your honor. He will take a string of lovers, sometimes weeping into their naked breasts: *Oh, I miss her so much.*

*There, there,* your husband's lovers will say, patting him on the head like a child. *There, there.*

Your husband's lovers will admire his devotion, will nod thoughtfully when their friends quote from his poetry: *I want to be loved like that.*

When reporters interview your husband, they'll say: *Tell us about your first wife.*

*Oh, where can I begin?* your husband will say. *Where can I begin?*

Your husband's second wife and third and fourth will never compare to you. You will be an angel; you will be a saint. *Maybe a little too rigid in bed*, your husband will confide to the lover the third wife will leave him over, the lover who will become the fourth wife.

Your husband's wives — second, third and fourth — will have to endure the photographs of you your husband will put up round the house. He'll have so many of them framed after your death. His favorite will be the one of you with a wineglass in your hand, head tossed back, laughing, surrounded by his friends.

*I must have said something frightfully clever,* your husband will say, *to make her laugh so hard.*

Your children will come to stay with your husband and the third wife when they're older. The second wife won't last long before she leaves your husband. What she had found charming in her bed, she will find less charming in his. The way he will still weep your name, keep your wedding photo on the bedstand table. The second wife will never learn your children's names, never select Christmas presents for them. The second wife will leave quietly, while your husband is gone for a reading, taking some of your jewelry when she goes. Your husband will bring lawsuit after lawsuit against her. She will always claim the jewelry was given as a gift.

The third wife will be awkward with your children at first, but then grow to love them. They'll be surprised at the weight of her arms the first time she embraces them, will think: *Is this what a mother feels like?*

The third wife will say: *I would never want to replace your mother.*

She and your children will be surrounded by the framed pictures of you. When they're eating, when they're watching television. You will always be there. The third wife will develop a nervous habit of smoothing her hair when she glances at the photo of you holding the wine glass, laughing. One day, when there is a sudden gust of wind, that photo will fall off the wall and be torn on the glass shards. Your husband and the third wife will have their first argument.

*You did this on purpose,* he'll say.

*I know how much she means to you,* the third wife will cry.

Your children will flee to their bedrooms. The third wife will follow them later and apologize.

*Your father is a great man,* she'll say. *It's all thanks to your mother.*

After the third wife leaves your husband, he'll move the fourth wife into the house. His friends will never approve of her. *That little twist he married,* they'll call her. The fourth wife won't be so stupid she wouldn't notice. She'll pour glasses of wine at your husband's dinner parties with trembling, furious hands. She'll let some of it spill onto the counter, leave it till morning, let it stain. She'll want to put some of the photographs into storage — that one where your face is half-covered in shadow, where your shirt has slipped off one shoulder, especially — but your husband will tell her it has to stay. *They all have to stay.*

The fourth wife will be the youngest of all his wives, except for you, married to your husband just out of high school, both of you *so young then, so vibrant,* he'll say. The fourth wife won't be as pretty as the second wife or as kind as the third, but she'll be young. And she will dust your framed photos every week, though she hates them, hates you, perfect, unaging, *murdered,* because your husband is a great man.

## Being the Murdered Lover

The thing about being the murdered lover is you set the plot in motion.

Your lover will be suspected, investigated. His wife and her three fur coats. Ermine, ermine, ermine.

Your lover's wife will burn one of her ermine coats after it's returned to her from the police, the one they took as evidence, the one that covered your naked body. Set a bonfire in the back yard, even with her refined, thin hands, she can do something like that. Throw the ermine coat atop it, lips drawn back in a smile or a snarl. She'll be drunk on red wine, the kind your lover liked to save for special occasions.

The police will be called back to the house after the bonfire when the neighbors complain about the shouting and the thumping, the sound of broken things.

Your lover will be head in hands on the couch when the police come, his wife standing over him in a silk nightgown, clutching torn, burnt pieces of ermine: *How could you do this to us?*

*I'm sorry,* your lover will say. The police will take this as a confession. The police will think your lover murdered you to keep you quiet.

The police will think of you as a blackmailer, as a greedy, grasping woman. The police will see your naked body, reveal it from the fur coat, examine the ligature marks on your throat, think of their own wives, their own lovers. Will think: *Poor thing got what she deserved.*

Your lover will be taken away in handcuffs from his home. You had only been there twice, when his wife and her favorite ermine coat were gone, and he took you on their bed, where he said he hadn't touched his wife in years. You stared up at the ceiling and clutched the sheets in your hands. Later, he draped you in the ermine coat that would later cover your dead body, said: *A girl like you deserves nice things.*

While your lover is sitting in his holding cell in a fine Italian suit, his wife will pack a suitcase, unpack it, pack it again.

Your lover will call his lawyer; his wife will call hers. The lawyers will say: *Don't tell them anything.* The lawyers will say: *Let me do the talking.* The lawyers will both secretly suspect their client of being guilty. The lawyers will file motions and snap their briefcases open and closed, clatter down courthouse hallways in their dress shoes.

Your photograph will be brought out from time to time. There will be two the police like to use in their investigation, the first a selfie they downloaded from your phone, duck-lipped, squinting.

*Do you recognize this woman?* they'll say, and follow it up with the one of you dead and naked on the floor, draped in an ermine coat.

*Do you recognize her now?*

The police will secretly prefer the photo of you dead, find something attractive in the parting of your lips, the bruising of your throat, something graceful in your death, something fragile, something precious.

In the first photo, you aren't making duck lips at all. You are blowing a kiss.

*Kiss me,* your lover texted you. *I want you to kiss me.*

*I'll look silly,* you said.

*Please,* he said. *Please.*

The police will box up your belongings, return them to your roommate after your funeral.

*What kind of girl was she?* they'll say.

*Nice,* your roommate will say. *Quiet.*

Your roommate will never be a suspect. Your roommate will read about the investigation in the newspaper whenever there is any progress. Your roommate will, in time, forget your middle name.

People will say to your roommate: *Didn't you used to live with her? That woman who was murdered?*

Your roommate won't mind the question, except once, when she is about to get married, getting fitted for her dress, the bridal shop employee spreading measuring tape over her body: *Didn't you used to live with that woman who was murdered?*

And your roommate, arms crossed over her bare breasts, will begin to cry. The tears will surprise her; she'll wipe them away with one hand, keep the other over her breasts, assume she is oversensitive because of her impending wedding.

*No,* she'll say. *I never knew her.*

The investigation will drag on for years. Your lover's wife will keep the suitcase under her bed, *just in case*, will keep a bed of her own, a room of her own, sit across from her husband at dinners out on the town to keep up appearances, introduce herself to important people: *Oh, that was all just a terrible misunderstanding. We hope things will be cleared up soon.*

Your lover's wife will smile a tight-lipped smile. Your lover's wife will become so proficient at this tight-lipped smile. She'll wake in her bed in the night, smiling that smile, touch the corners of her mouth in the dark, think of you.

*You didn't have to die,* she'll say when the newspaper runs their articles on the anniversary of your death, say to the duck-lipped photo of you on the front page. *You didn't have to do this to me.*

Your lover's wife will hate herself for thinking this, dig her manicured nails into her palms. She will smile over the top of the newspaper at her husband, that practiced, tight-lipped smile.

*Please pass the salt,* she'll say, and make certain, when he does, that their hands don't brush.

# Being the Murdered Actress

The thing about being the murdered actress is you set the plot in motion.

Your picture will be in the tabloids, your parted mouth, your half-closed eyes. *She was so beautiful,* people will say. *So young.* You'll be loved, desperately. Photos of you cut out of magazines, pasted on bedroom walls; your name tattooed onto forearms, upper thighs. *I'll never forget her.*

They'll write a biopic about you. A man will. A man who knew you, tangentially, when you were still alive. A man who remembers, tangentially, the sound of your laughter, the tap of your footstep. He'll write you the way he remembers you, the way the people do. He'll write you larger than life.

In your death, you will be larger than life. Like a face on a movie screen.

The tabloids will announce the production of the biopic. They'll look for the perfect girl. Starlets will line up for auditions in red lipstick, spike heels. They'll all have their hair styled like yours. They'll have watched your films as research, research, even your earliest films, where you didn't have any lines, filled in the background, stood, sat, walked, smiled, looked pretty.

*What's my motivation,* you used to ask your directors.

*Be sexy,* they said. *Be soda pop and apple pie.*

That's what they'll tell the starlets in line, twisting in their heeled shoes, rubbing the backs of their necks.

*Be soda pop,* the starlets will agree, think of bubbles, think of fizz, think of the snap of aluminum coming undone.

There will be a girl on the stage. The girl on the stage will be speaking lines from your most famous movie. The girl on the stage will be inhabiting you to the smallest of her gestures.

*She's the one,* the whisper will go down through the line of starlets, *she's the one.*

The producers will be nodding, the director. *She's the one, yes,* nodding, thinking how well they knew you, how well everyone did.

The girl on the stage will finish speaking her lines, *your* lines. The girl on the stage will feel their eyes on her. The girl on the stage will feel like you, feel loved, feel like you. Will bow, say: *How was I?*

When the girl from the stage is cast in your biopic, the tabloids will begin to call her by your name. Her own name will be gone. *Our new girl,* they will call her, *our new beloved one.* The girl with your name will look in the mirror sometimes, see your face.

*Is this me?* she'll say.

The girl with your name will film your death scene first.

*We have to see if you can handle it,* the producers will say. *The rest will be cake.*

*Easy as pie,* the producers will say.

The girl with your name will never understand why the producers always talk food, *soda pop, apple pie.*

*Are they so hungry,* she'll say to the makeup artist in your voice.

The producers will have the death scene shot again and again, watch the daily rushes, shake their heads.

*It needs to be more real,* they'll say.

*We need to believe it,* they'll say.

The director will ask for different angles, for less lighting, more lighting. The director will kneel beside the girl with your name, playing dead on the concrete floor, sheer black teddy, restrain her shivering body.

*Every actress wants to play a death scene,* the director will say.

He'll grab the girl with your name by her thin wrist. It will be like grabbing you. He never touched you, not when you were alive. He'll think it would have been like touching her now. He'll pull her off the concrete floor by that one wrist and the girl with your name will think how it is, the difference between the two of them, his hand, her wrist, will think *is this how she felt*, will think, *yes, this is how she felt.*

The girl with your name will film the death scene. She'll knock it out of the park, the producers will say, *you knocked it out of the park,* shake her hand, linger with their touch. The girl with your name will be magnificent, the girl with your name will smile, smile, smile. The tabloids will say how she is you now, how she is just like you.

# Being the Murdered Coed

The thing about being the murdered coed is you set the plot in motion.

You won't be found for days after, leaves dropping onto your body from shedding autumn trees. You will be nearly buried under them. Left on a part of campus no one ever goes, you'll be found by a woman walking a very small dog. The woman will be wearing purple leggings, shoes with matching laces. The very small dog will pick up your scent. The very small dog will bark, will bark, will bark.

Your parents will be called. Your parents will make arrangements for a closed casket funeral. The university will release a statement filled with platitudes and obfuscations. They'll hire an additional security guard to walk the campus at night, flashlight in hand. He'll lean up against the brick of the library building, smoke e-cigarettes flavored like mangoes. He'll look up at the sky from time to time, admire the fat of the moon when it's full.

The police will interview everyone from the party where you were last seen. The police won't blame you for your own murder, not really, but they'll think if you had maybe been *more careful.*

You had a beer. You had a beer. You had another. You had hair in need of trimming and a laugh that turned into a duck quack if it went on too long. You had sex. You had shoes left from high school tucked under your bed, black lace panties in your dresser, purple lace panties, champagne lace panties.

The police will make note of this, note of the signs of trauma to your body, note of your unblemished fingernails, that you didn't fight back, that you didn't even *try.*

*When did she leave the party?*

But nobody noticed you leave, nobody noticed anybody paying an excessive amount of attention to you. They'll remember you had beer, they'll remember you were slurring your speech. They'll remember one of the foreign students on the basketball team said he had you the weekend before, *had you* the way you had a beer and another and another. You sat behind the basketball player in World Lit. He had a wart beside his left ear, pale skin, bad haircut. He stuttered his left foot against the desk in front of him, wore a scarf even when it was warm.

The police will interview him for hours, his English faltering with his nerves: *Just once, that's all. The just once time.*

But he was still at the party after you were gone, they'll say, so it couldn't have been him.

Your mother will think he followed you later, murdered you later. Your mother will have an immense distrust of foreigners since her childhood, your mother will vote for politicians who want to build walls, your mother will mourn loudly, clacking up and down the hallway of your childhood home in her heels. She'll think *I want to go somewhere*, she'll think *where could I go,* she'll reach the end of the hallway, turn around, ankles throbbing. She'll go back and forth, back and forth, tap, tap, tap.

Your mother will be shamed to know you had sex. Your mother will be shamed to know you kissed a girl at the party, Wendy Chin, thin lips soft under yours, mouth tasting of beer, the both of you breathing faster, faster, touching soft shoulders with soft fingertips, until one of the guys said *god, that's hot,* and you broke apart and you didn't speak to Wendy Chin again, didn't look at Wendy Chin again.

Wendy Chin will say she doesn't remember kissing you before you died.

Wendy Chin will say *I was drunk, we were drunk, she was drunk, everyone was drunk.*

Wendy Chin will marry a boy with a Subaru Outback. Wendy Chin will have three children and join a book club. She'll start drinking wine instead of beer. She'll have no taste for it, drink it like she's taking a shot.

Wendy Chin will, from time to time, think of you. The basketball player never will. He'll forget your name before he even returns to his home country, call you *the girl that was murdered* when he calls you anything, will forget he *had* you, will forget *you.*

The new security guard will stay on campus for seven months, till the funding dries up, till the curl of your dead hand, half-covered by leaves, is forgotten.

The woman and the very small dog will take a different route on their walks. The woman will think of you sometimes, like Wendy Chin, think of you, sigh *what a waste,* and lean back in her recliner, her very small dog resting quiet at her feet, dreaming of dead things.

# Being the Murdered Clerk

*For M.F.*

The thing about being the murdered clerk is you set the plot in motion.

You'll be found by passersby at the end of your shift, half-in, half-out of the shop, door propped open by your hollowed body. They'll check for your pulse, they'll run for the nearest phone. They'll note the curl and clutch of your fingers, how you must have dragged yourself to the door. They'll say *she fought so hard.* They'll say *she wanted to live.*

You'll be found. Your killer never will. There will be a reward for information, posters with your name, your face. Pinned up at the post office, at grocery stores, on telephone poles: *$5,000 Reward.* Everyone will know your face, the dark of your hair, slant of your near-smile. Yours will be the face parents know better than the faces of their own daughters; yours will be the name uttered in cautions from mothers buttoning their children into autumn jackets.

*Be careful,* they'll say. *Oh, be careful.*

Over the years, the reward will grow. Your parents will put money in, your boss, local business owners, police associations: ten, fifteen, twenty. Your face will stay the same on the posters, your name. You are unchanging and dead. You will be, always, unchanging and dead.

Your parents will forget the sound of your voice, scent of your favorite perfume, gone stale in its bottle, perched on your bureau in your empty room. Your mother will stand in the middle of your room from time to time, touch your things with a brush of her knuckles, lightly, lightly, try to evoke you with a calling of your name.

A reporter will call your parents for an interview in honor of the ten-year anniversary of your death. She'll be new to town, print a copy of your reward poster for her notes. The receptionist was a girl when you were killed; the receptionist will see the poster on the printer, run her fingertip over your face.

*Oh,* she'll say, curve of fingernail caressing the flat of your printed hair. *Oh, I remember her.*

The reporter will go to your parents' house. They'll show her your bedroom, wrinkle of your bedspread, clutter of your closet. The pieces of you that have been left behind: favorite books, high-heeled sandals, teddy bear missing one button eye.

*We thought it would be safe here,* they'll say. *We thought it couldn't happen here.*

Your parents are from out of town, and you were, and your little brothers. Moved from the big city to the small town, the *everybody-knows-your-name* town. Your old classmates will never hear of your death when it happens, will wonder from time to time, *whatever happened to her*, will enter your name in search engines, will find your face, will see *Reward for Information*, will say: *Oh, I remember her.*

The reporter will write a series of articles about your murder that will go on to win a statewide journalism award. The reporter will collect your posters as they're released: fifteen, twenty, twenty-five. You will be the ghost haunting the reporter, the name she brings up again, again, again.

On the fifteenth anniversary of your death, the reporter will think of calling your parents, *for old time's sake,* she'll think, hover her hand over the phone. She won't dial. She'll go to a dive bar down the street when her shift is over at midnight. She'll drink too many beers, spill some on the cuff of her paisley shirt. She'll go home with a retired cop, one who knows you too, the way the town knows you, toast in your honor, say your name. She'll go home with the retired cop, wake in his bed in the dark, the unfamiliarity of his breath against her neck, roll away from him, curl herself into a ball, think of your weary eyes.

The next day, she'll cut her hair, shorter than it's ever been.

*You look so pretty,* her coworkers will say. *You look so young.*

The reporter will smile slantwise, say *thank you, thank you,* looking like a reflection of you.

The reporter will leave the newspaper abruptly and never return, taking all but one of your posters with her. They'll sit in the passenger seat of her car; she'll drive and drive and drive until the town is lost behind her. She'll drop your posters in trash bins along the way, till she gets to the last one, think *no,* think *no, no, no,* tuck it into the trunk of her car, where it will stay.

The poster left behind will remain taped to the wall by the reporter's desk, covered and covered by notes. The receptionist will have to clean out the reporter's desk for her replacement, will see the corner of the reward poster. She'll lift the notes away with the tips of her fingers, delicate, barely moving them at all. She won't need to move them much to know it's you.

*Oh,* she'll say, touch your chin with her fingertips. *Oh, I remember her.*

# Being the Murdered Homecoming Queen

The thing about being the murdered homecoming queen is you set the plot in motion.

You'll be a haunt long after your name is forgotten; you'll be famous. You'll be summoned at impromptu after-school séances in the gymnasium, girls sitting lotus-style, knees brushing, cupping flashlights under their chins, wearing gossamer scarves, smelling of their mothers' incense and potpourri.

*I can feel her,* they'll say, one to another. *I can feel her presence.*

One girl will speak in tongues, writhe, faint. The other girls will wake her with delicate splashes from water bottles, flicked from their fingertips: *Are you possessed now? Are you her?*

The girl who fainted will only be herself, and they will all sigh with disappointment, tiptoe out of the gym before the custodian comes by.

You'll be a picture in the yearbook memoriam section, next to the cancer kid, next to the boy who ran the stop sign, next to a trite poem about loss.

You'll be a ghost, a ghost, a ghost.

The girls will remember you, the girls always will. Pass you down from one class to another, lose your name along the way. Murdered homecoming queen, you don't need a name, the thing you have become is more real a name than the one you ever had before.

You'll be a ghost for the girls alone. You'll be red-lipsticked backwards writing on the bathroom mirror, cold spot in the hallway outside the science lab, flicker of band room lights at 1:43 p.m. every other Thursday.

You'll be the curse on the other homecoming queens, girls holding their bodies away from their kings for the shared homecoming dance, girls sharp-elbowed and stiff, heavy head in tiara.

The girls will whisper you, scratch your existence into the tops of desks, bathroom stall doors. You will be larger and more real than you ever used to be. You will envelop the school.

The girls, the girls, the girls.

They'll keep you, even as women, keep you as their first ghost, keep your sadness, tuck it against themselves at night, between them and their husbands, kiss it into their daughters' foreheads.

*A murdered homecoming queen could never be happy,* they'll tell the nodding daughters.

*All that,* they'll say, *taken away,* and the daughters will say *yes, all that,* dream of rhinestone tiaras clattering against concrete, tap of heels dyed to match homecoming dress, glare of spotlight, bundle of roses. Dream of you. The daughters will wake; the daughters will walk the hallways you used to walk; the daughters will keep you too, always, always, always.

# Being the Murdered Teacher

The thing about being the murdered teacher is you set the plot in motion.

The children will cry when they're told. Even Gavin Fire Crow, tallest fourth grader, with his nearly-a-man's shoulders, he'll cry, the tears slipping quiet down the sides of his face. The girls will huddle around Starla Mark with her uneven pigtails, drag their desks into a circle where the boys aren't welcome.

Their weeping sounds like the swirling of water at the base of a waterfall, the principal will think, standing at the front of the classroom with the substitute teacher who'd been filling in for you while they searched.

The principal will have waterfalls on his mind. You will be found beside the small one just outside of town. We will be curled like a leaf husk, your cardigan torn, your shoes missing.

*Where are her shoes,* the principal will say when the police notify him. He won't remember saying it; he won't have any reason for saying it other than he doesn't like the thought of your stockinged feet in the dirt.

Before the police notify the principal, they'll tell your wife. They'll go to your house, two of them, a short one and a tall one — *Mutt and Jeff,* your wife's mother will say, peering out the front window. *They look like Mutt and Jeff.*

Your wife will be washing dishes when she is told. When the two police say to her, *would you like to stop, would you like to sit down,* she'll say, *no, I can't stop,* her hands covered in suds, scrub the same dish the entire time they are saying *we've found her, we're sorry.*

Your wife will rinse the dish, her back to the police. She'll turn to face them while she dries, present them a crackling smile.

*Can I offer you some tea?*

Your wife's mother will be standing just outside the kitchen; your wife's mother will have heard everything.

*Honey,* she'll say, come rushing in, embrace her daughter. *Honey, let me get the tea.*

*Honey,* she'll say, *can't you please sit?*

*No, I can't please sit,* your wife will say, go back to washing that same dish while her mother starts the water in the teakettle boiling.

Your wife will go to the school after your death. She'll try to guess the children from your descriptions of them, standing outside the chain-link fence, looking in at the playground. She'll only know Gavin Fire Crow from his broad shoulders.

The principal will come outside with the custodian when the teacher on recess duty reports a stranger watching the children. The principal won't recognize your wife at first until she says, *I came to get her things.*

*Of course,* the principal will say, dismiss the custodian, take your wife by the elbow.

The substitute will be in your classroom, erasing equations from the whiteboard. The substitute will stay on until a full-time replacement is hired; the substitute will go home at night to her own family, make dinner like they expect, tell them about her day.

*It was fine,* she'll say.

She'll never tell them anything more. They'll never ask.

The substitute will be there when your wife comes for your things, children outside for recess. She'll be erasing the whiteboard, be thinking of buying pepper spray for her teenage daughter, be thinking of telling her *there are wolves.*

Your wife will hesitate at the doorway of your classroom. Your wife's eyes will be red from crying.

*I came to get her things,* she'll say, and the substitute will startle, thinking *there are wolves, there are wolves, there are wolves,* drop the eraser on the floor.

*I'm sorry,* she'll say, *I'm sorry, you were just so quiet.*

The substitute will retrieve your things in their box behind the coat closet, press them into your wife's arms. Your wife will curve under the weight of the box. Your things won't be that heavy at all, but to your wife, they will feel like they are.

*The children loved her so much,* the substitute will say. *So much.*

*Thank you,* your wife will say. *Thank you, thank you,* prop your things against her hip, carry them out to her car.

The children will be on the playground, the children will be laughing the laughter of children. Your wife will watch them from the other side of the chain link fence. She'll see Gavin Fire Crow playing tetherball, the breadth of his shoulders, will call out to him by name. He won't hear her, and the other tetherball players will say *Gavin, hey, Gavin, some lady's calling you,* but by the time he turns to look, your wife will already be walking away.

# Being the Murdered Babysitter

The thing about being the murdered babysitter is you set the plot in motion.

Your geometry homework will still be on the Harrisons' coffee table, a boy's name written on the grocery-bag cover, traced again and again with black pen.

Mrs. Harrison came home tipsy, she'll say *tipsy*, husband's arms supporting her, giggling like a girl, tangled hair catching on her wedding ring. She won't remember if you were still there when they returned, won't remember if you needed a ride from Mr. Harrison or if you said you'd walk, sometimes you did that, just a couple blocks away, quiet neighborhood, safe.

*It was our anniversary,* Mrs. Harrison will say. *We were celebrating.*

*The kids loved her,* she'll say.

You drew them pictures of horses that they pinned to their walls, taught them how to swear in Japanese.

After your death, the Harrison children will say *kuso, kuso*, ride ghost horses through the house. Mrs. Harrison will think she hears the beating of hooves, touch Mr. Harrison's forearm, *do you hear that?*

*It's just the children,* he'll say.

Mr. Harrison will be interrogated for hours, *interrogated,* Mrs. Harrison will say, left hand twitching, *like a criminal.*

He'll say he gave you a ride. He'll say he let you off at home.

The police will push Styrofoam cups of steaming coffee across the table to him. The police will talk to him like equals, like friends. One will have a wife in the PTA at the Harrison children's school.

*Did you wait to see if she got inside?*

Mr. Harrison will say *yes*, will say *I think so*, will finally say *I don't remember.*

*I had a glass of wine,* he'll say. *Maybe two.*

He'll say: *I probably shouldn't have been driving.*

When the police talk to your parents, your mother will say: *My baby.* She'll say *my baby, my baby, my baby.* The youngest of your four older brothers will sit on a bench at the station beside her. He'll blink and blink and chew on a stick of gum from your mother's purse. He'll stay seated on the bench when the police come out with Mr. Harrison, when your mother throws herself at him like they do on television, beat her hands against his chest, *my baby.*

Mr. Harrison won't be able to look at your mother, won't be able to step away from her tiny, flailing fists. Mr. Harrison will try to say *I'm sorry, I'm sorry*, but his mouth will only open and close without a sound.

Mrs. Harrison will do the laundry after your death, run the linens through the wash again, again, again.

*Do these smell musty to you?* she'll ask Mr. Harrison.

Mr. Harrison will say they don't smell like anything at all.

*I'll wash them one more time,* Mrs. Harrison will say, *just in case.*

She'll fold the sheets in the youngest Harrison child's bedroom, keep an eye on the drawings of horses pinned to the wall. She'll think how alive they seem, as if the paper is only barely holding them back. She'll remember how much her children loved horses after you started babysitting, how the youngest told her the names of the ones in the drawings: Charley Chase, Marion Davies, Max Linder. She'll think the names are familiar, think maybe they were people once, long ago.

The youngest Harrison child will come back to her room, find Mrs. Harrison still there, folding and refolding sheets.

*These horses,* Mrs. Harrison will say. *Are they real horses?*

Mrs. Harrison will swear she can hear hoofbeats, will say to her youngest: *You hear it too?*

Mrs. Harrison will think of the name written on your geometry book, the dedication inherent in the tracing.

*She must have done it every day,* she'll say to her book club, goblet of red wine in her hand.

*She must have been,* Mrs. Harrison will say, *so in love.*

Mrs. Harrison will hear the beating of hooves, Mrs. Harrison will be beset by phantom horses, will insist on taking down every one of your drawings from her youngest's room, over the child's protests, march them out to the garbage.

*It's not horses,* Mr. Harrison will say after rescuing the drawings in the evening, smoothing them out, laying them on the youngest Harrison child's bed.

*What is it, then,* Mrs. Harrison will say, and her husband will put his hand to her chest, and she will feel his warmth, feel her own racing heart, the way her pulse is pounding in her ears.

# Being the Murdered Bride

The thing about being the murdered bride is you set the plot in motion.

Everyone will remember the blossoming of red on your ivory dress, the limpness of your neck. The best man's hands will come away covered with blood; the groom's mother will scream; your maid of honor will drop her bouquet, grip the hem of her dress, tug, tug, tug.

The flower girl will have nightmares about blooming posies. She will have a terror of red roses, white roses, in-between pinks. When she is older, for Valentine's Day, she will tear petals off of flowers, say, *no,* say *I don't want those, I hate them, no,* ask for chocolates in heart-shaped boxes, cactuses in ceramic pots.

After you have been killed, the groom's mother will scream and scream.

She thought of you as a daughter, the daughter she never had. She paid for the highlights in your hair, took you on lunch dates, promised her son he had chosen the right woman.

*She'll make you happy.*

Afterwards, the groom's mother will wait alone in the fellowship hall, open a bottle of champagne, let it bubble out over her fingers. She'll pour it into one of the cheap plastic goblets, drink, pour, drink again, again. Her throat will be ragged from the screaming. She'll have to whisper her answers to the police, champagne-breathed.

*What did you see?*

*A man with a gun.*

Your blood will leave a stain on the carpet by the altar. Days later, the minister will try to remove it with baking soda and ice cubes.

*Isn't that for bee stings, though,* the church pianist will say, standing beside him in her sensible shoes, her navy skirt.

*I don't know,* the minister will say, rubbing the ice into the carpet, *I don't know, I have to do something.*

Your blood will remain after the wedding, after your death. The church membership will be dwindling; there will only be enough in the collection plate for a rug that the minister will lay over the place you died. He will always step around the rug, always inhale sharply when someone else walks on it.

He'll say *don't,* he'll say *don't,* reach his hand for the bible on his lectern, say *please.*

Your maid of honor will come by the church sometimes, after your death, sit in the parking lot in her compact car, tires nudged up against the curb. She'll want to go in, maybe at least go up to the door, but she won't. She'll stay in her car, play the radio too loud. She'll learn the words to all the pop songs, sing them with the window down.

Your maid of honor will embark on a brief affair with your husband-to-be. The maid of honor will hate herself for this betrayal, hate herself as your husband-to-be kisses her throat, her collarbone. He'll hate himself, too, the way he says she resembles you, the way he says *you're just like her, you could have been sisters, you're so much alike*. Says it until your maid of honor bursts into tears, rolls away, dresses at the edge of his bed, *we're not the same, I'm not her, we're not the same.*

*I know,* your husband-to-be will say. *I know, it's not what I meant.*

He'll reach out for your maid of honor; she'll flinch from his touch.

He'll say: *I'm sorry.*

He'll say: *I'm sorry, I'm sorry,* the way he did when you were murdered, kneeling beside your body, blood on his best friend's hands. *God, I'm sorry.*

After their affair is over, your maid of honor will finally be able to enter the church where you were killed. Pull up to the curb in her compact car. She'll swipe through photos of you on her phone, she'll sing along with new pop songs that sound just like the old ones.

The minister will be there when your maid of honor climbs the church steps, opens the door.

The sun behind her, the minister will see her and think, for a moment, of you.

*Oh,* he'll say, *oh, don't I know you?*

Your maid of honor will look back toward her car, will take a step back toward her car.

*Don't I know you?* the minister will say.

She'll say: *No.*

She'll say: *No, I don't think you do.*

# Being the Murdered Moll

The thing about being the murdered moll is you set the plot in motion.

Rain will be falling when you die; they'll say rain was falling. They'll say you woke with a knot in the pit of your belly, tugged your lover's arm at the peek of sun through the hotel room curtain. They'll say it wasn't raining *yet*, it wasn't raining *then*.

Your lover will clutch your bullet-riddled body, they'll say *bullet-riddled*. He'll howl his rage to the storm clouds, vow vengeance in your name. He will become Romeo and you will be Juliet. You always wanted to be somebody, they'll say. You always wanted to be a star.

They'll say the night before, you sat up with your lover in the dark of a hotel room after convenience store robbery, suitcases stuffed with leaking liquor bottles, whiskey-sticky dollar bills. You gazed out the open curtain, knees tucked to chin. They'll say you were wearing your best dress the night before you died, say it was growing threadbare frayed, but you were still beautiful in it, still beautiful in a hard, hopeful way.

Sitting like that, they'll say, you looked out the window at the sky, your lover's fingers entwined with yours, *the stars,* you said to him, *the stars, the stars.*

*The stars envy us, don't they?*

And in the morning, they'll say, curtains drawn, slant of sunlight wisping across your face, you woke with a knot in your stomach, woke *knowing,* reached for your lover's arm.

It will be raining when you die, stolen car dragging in the back-road mud. They'll say there was a *pepper of gunfire*; they'll say you were wearing your best dress again, wearing it still, were smoothing the folds over your lap, looking out the window at the falling rain.

They'll say there was a gun on your lap, you were the kind of girl who'd carry a gun for your lover, say you were turning to your lover, opening your mouth to speak.

*Maybe,* you said, *maybe we could —*

The way the pepper of gunfire will punctuate the falling rain, the way he will cradle your body in the mud, the way he will rise up, guns blazing, they'll like that, *guns blazing*, the way he leaves you on the ground before he falls too, your mouth still parted in death from the last words you had spoken, your mouth still parted, waiting, waiting for your Romeo's kiss.

# Being the Murdered Professor

The thing about being the murdered professor is you set the plot in motion.

Your husband will have you buried in one of those pastel pantsuits you always wore. He'll say *she loved this one,* he'll think you loved pantsuits, really think you did.

He'll find a minister for your service that one of your colleagues recommends, *did my father's service, everyone loved him.* He'll sit down with the minister in your kitchen, unwashed dishes in the sink, crumpled napkin by the stove. Your husband will crumple another napkin while he and the minister discuss your services, wad it up, smooth it out, over and over again.

The minister will say soothing things. The minister will have a firm grip when he shakes your husband's hand. He'll suggest scriptures, hymns, an order of service.

*It's best to do these things in a certain way,* he'll say.

The minister will shake your husband's hand again before he goes, leave your husband feeling comforted, feeling known.

Your five nephews will sit with your husband in the mortuary chapel for your service. They'll leave their wives and children at home.

Your youngest niece-in-law will be pregnant with a third child, will want to attend, remember you from Thanksgiving dinners and Christmas eves, your perfect posture, your unflinching smile. How you offered her a shot of brandy in a Santa-decorated paper cup once, *to get through the holiday, you know*, laughed.

*I liked her,* your niece-in-law will say. *I want to go.*

Your nephew will pat her rounded belly, rub her head like she's one of their daughters. Your nephew will have a habit of patting his wife on the head, won't notice when she begins flinching away. Your nephew will be hoping this one is a boy.

*It will be too stressful,* he'll say. *You should stay home with the girls.*

Your five nephews will sit on either side of your husband, pass tissues to him in the middle, tell him he's being strong, so very strong.

The minister will stand at the front of the chapel. He'll barely need the microphone clipped to his lapel, his voice rising like riverflow. He'll read the words of Matthew, Mark, John, Paul. He'll say *this song was written by a man who lost everything*, have the congregation sing *It Is Well With My Soul*. The minister will relate to your death through the words of men, the minister will fill the chapel with the words of men.

You will be at the front of the chapel too, in a casket chosen to match your pastel pantsuit. You'll be locked away, closed away, hidden behind stands and stands of flowers. The casket spray will be provided by the university, soft and sweet, lilacs and daisies; your husband will cry when he sees it.

*It's beautiful,* he'll say. *It's so beautiful.*

Your husband will shake hands with your colleagues. They'll tell him you were *a real go-getter, a real ballbuster.*

*That sounds terrible,* they'll say. *She'd have loved it. You know how she was. Just one of the guys.*

Your colleagues will meet after your service for a glass of beer at the bar nearest campus. They won't go to your burial, won't want to see you *lowered into the ground*, won't be able to, the one who's known you the longest will say, *bear it*. One of them will write a poem about your burial later, as if he had been there, really. He'll use lilacs as a metaphor for your femininity, daisies as a metaphor for death. He'll win an award, keep it in his office for students to admire.

Your colleague poet will raise a glass of beer in your honor, loosen his tie. All your colleagues will loosen their ties at the bar nearest campus, all of them will say *cheers*, say *here's to a real ballbuster of a gal.*

The minister will be speaking at your grave. He'll say *think of all the things she has taught us. Think of what we have learned from her, about God.*

Your husband will dip his head at this, wipe at his eyes with one of the tissues your nephews gave him. On the ground before him, he'll see a stem-snapped lilac, crouch to pick it up, cup it in the palm of his hands, think how fragile it is, how very fragile.

# Being the Murdered Student

The thing about being the murdered student is you set the plot in motion.

You'll be late for dinner. Your baby sister and your father will eat without you, quiet except the hum of the corner fan, your mother leaving her plate and yours bare, dinner covered on the stove. Your mother will see sparrows in the yard; the yard will be blanketed by sparrows, and she'll tap her finger against the window, breath fogging the glass, think *collective nouns*, think *knot, quarrel, flutter*. She'll hear your name in the whisper of their chirping mouths, feel the beginning of something leaving the inside of her, a hollowing in her chest, and the phone will ring.

When the phone rings, the sparrows will take flight, all at once, rush of wing clap, shout of feather, and your mother will watch them empty from the yard, hand pressed to chest, trying to hold that hollowing in.

She'll answer the phone — your baby sister will be practicing her viola lesson and your father never picks up after seven — and when the man on the other end of the line identifies himself as Det. Mulvaney and says: *I'm sorry*, your mother will hang up reflexively.

Your mother will hang up the phone and begin to keen, wail until she can barely breathe, until only the gasping hollow in her chest is left, and your baby sister will lay down her viola and your father will mute the television and, again, the telephone will ring.

Your plate will be bare on the table, the knife and fork and spoon your pouting baby sister laid out nestled against each other. Your mother will scoop them all up in one hand, drop them into the dishwasher with everything else, run the dishwasher, settle into its rhythmic hum, say *God,* say *God,* say *God* again.

Your baby sister will leave her viola on the bench beside her, bump her elbow against it when she goes for her phone, texts her friends: *My sister, my sister.*

Your baby sister will leave the viola on the bench all night, will fall asleep on the hardwood floor beneath it, kidney bean- curled, phone in one hand, other hand fist-tucked under her chin. She'll wake sore. She'll think of going to school, she'll remember the sound of the ringing telephone, how she has always hated it, how she would, and you would, pick it up and slam it back down when your parents weren't home, over and over, until the calling finally stopped. Your baby sister will drag her bow across the viola's neck, will play something by Brahms after those first yowling morning notes, *Sonata in E-flat Major*, eyes closed, going up on tiptoes.

Your mother will be standing in the kitchen, standing all night, emptied dishwasher door open, how many times she ran into it with her shins in the night putting dishes away, how her legs are covered in bruises, one thick welt, how she still didn't shut the door. How she ran the vegetable peeler over the knuckles of her left hand, how she thought *replace her pain with mine, replace her pain with mine,* how she said *God God God,* how it was really a prayer.

And your father will be still in the den, wake to the sound of Brahms, stiff-necked couch-sleeping, realize the television has been playing all night: the sunshine smiles of the morning newscasters, the steaming cups of coffee on their desks.

He will go to the kitchen and your baby sister will go, and your mother will be there at the window, left hand cold-rinsed clean, right hand, right side of her face pressed to the glass, watch her breath become fog there.

*Look,* she'll say.

*Look, the sparrows have returned.*

# Being the Murdered Princess

The thing about being the murdered princess is you set the plot in motion.

They'll have parades for you, they'll light candles. Vigils in community parks, on courthouse lawns. Little girls in tiaras and black armbands.

*Our princess,* they'll all weep, *our princess.*

You had always belonged to them, *princess*, even more now that you have been murdered. They will call you *ours, ours, ours.*

There will be commemorative issues of magazines published. There will be your face smiling out from newsstands, drugstore racks, grocery shopping carts.

There will be girls who dreamed of being you, women now, with jobs and uncomfortable shoes and dogs that sleep on the couch. They'll remember how they played with their dolls and pretended to be you, the prince doll kissing the princess doll, the prince doll saving the princess doll, the prince doll taking her, taking her away, taking her away from all this.

*Why are you crying?* their husbands will say at dinner.

*Oh, was I crying?* the girls will say, wipe at their eyes. *I didn't think I was crying.*

The television stations will replay your last interview. The way you crossed your legs demurely, the way your posture was perfect, the way your smile *soothed.*

*She was so full of life,* they'll say.

They'll light candles for you again, the anniversary of your death, over and over, again. They'll hold the candles till they are burnt away, make wishes on the melt of wax curdling in their hands. Wish for a world with no more dead princesses, a world where you would have been queen.

*She would have made a wonderful queen,* they'll say.

The queen, though, will never die. The queen will live for a hundred years. The queen will flake and curl like parchment paper, never, never die.

The queen will be there every year on the anniversary of your death, lower her head, wear a black gown. The queen will have a special designer to make a new black gown every year, the queen will have a stylist to select the perfect muted shade of lipstick.

The queen never loved you; queen will never say your name.

The queen will step out on the palace balcony, lower her head. The queen will have shimmering eyes, looking like she might weep. It will only be a trick of the light. She will raise her head after a moment, to speak. She will be, they'll say, *majestic*.

*Thank you,* the queen will say to the crowds gathered outside the palace, their candles flickering away, melting away, going dark. *Thank you all.*

And when they go home, plucking candle melt from their fingertips, seeing your face in the open magazines on their coffee tables, they will think of royalty. They will say: *I saw a queen.*

They'll say: *Today, I saw a queen.*

# Being the Murdered Mother

The thing about being the murdered mother is you set the plot in motion.

Your son will never love again, not the way he loved you, the first woman, the one who left. He'll date girls you wouldn't have approved of, girls who snap their gum, wear their skirts short. Tell himself you wouldn't approve of them. Tell himself they're nothing like you.

Your son will bring his girlfriends back to your house. He will think how empty it is now, fill the emptiness by playing the stereo too loud.

His father will say *turn that down*. His father will constantly be saying *turn that down*. Coming into the family room, feet heavy, *turn that down, it's too loud, turn that down,* your son and one of the girlfriends there, the girlfriends tugging down their shirts, adjusting the waist of their jeans.

The girlfriends will press themselves into the corner of your leather couch, try to hide away from your son and his father: *do you think your mother would like it, you acting like this*. The girlfriends will scratch their nails along the arm of the leather couch, tuck their feet underneath their bodies, make themselves small, small, small.

The girlfriends will regret getting involved with a boy who has lost his mother. They will think of it as *lost*, the way their own mothers say: *That poor boy. To lose his mother in such a way.*

The mothers will say to their daughters: *Why don't you invite him here for a nice, home-cooked meal?* and their daughters will shuffle their feet, shake their heads, make excuses, think of the leather couch, how it clung to their bare flesh, how your son kissed them desperately.

The last girlfriend will be the girl who always shows up late to school, doesn't always bother to brush her hair. Smokes unfiltered cigarettes, darkens her eyes amateurishly with black liner. Your son will see her standing outside at lunch to sneak a cigarette, will go outside to stand next to her.

*Bum a smoke?* will be his line.

The last girlfriend will have a mother, no father, *at least not one I ever met,* live in a tiny apartment, sleep on a pull-out bed.

She'll say: *Your mom died? That sucks.*

Your son will rub the back of his neck with his fist, something he has done since he was a child, how small his hands were when he was a child, how small his hands were before you were murdered.

*It does suck.*

The last girlfriend's mother, even in that tiny apartment, will make home-cooked meals, will say *you shouldn't smoke, it's bad for your health,* will touch her daughter comfortingly.

Your son and his father won't touch anymore, not like that. Your son and his father won't say your name anymore, tip family photos over on their faces, stare at the bare velvet backs of them.

The last girlfriend will say: *It feels haunted here.*

*Haunted,* your son will say, *haunted?*

The last girlfriend won't be able to express it, how the entire house is enveloped in an emptiness barer than the backs of photo frames. How the entire house is filled with the absence of you, and how your son is too.

She'll scratch her fingers on the arm of the leather couch, make herself small.

*You know,* she'll say.

The last girlfriend will be the sort of girl everyone expects to get murdered, ride in back seats of cars driven by strange boys, smoke cigarettes in dark alleys. The last girlfriend won't be like you at all. The last girlfriend will live forever.

Your son will turn on the stereo when she comes over, *I like this song, don't you.* She'll shrug, say *sure,* fish a cigarette out of her purse, tap it against the heel of her hand.

When your son's father comes in to say *turn that down,* she'll be outside on the back step, smoking, looking up at the starlit sky, and your son and his father will be, in the quiet of your house, alone.

## Being the Murdered Extra

The thing about being the murdered extra is you set the plot in motion.

You were a girl good at walking past cameras, background girl, corner-of-the-frame girl. Never-held-a-script girl, went-where-the-director-said girl.

You'll be found in an alley, it's always an alley for girls like you, didn't-quite-make-it girls, living-four-to-a-one-bedroom-apartment girls. You'll be found in an alley, you'll be mistaken for a broken mannequin at first, you'll be given a nickname. Blue Violet, White Rose, something reminiscent of Elizabeth Short, that first girl like you, that most famous one. The kind of dead girl who never really dies.

A color and a flower, a body in black lace dress, missing heels, missing purse. You'll be described by the things you have lost, by the things you almost were: wannabe starlet, wannabe model.

Your roommates will say you had a date that night. Your roommates will say you were always going on dates.

*She liked men, huh,* the cops will say.

*Who doesn't, right,* your roommates will sigh, drink the cheap coffee they're offered.

One of them, a girl from Wyoming, will handroll cigarettes and remember the prairie, remember what the moon looks like in a town uncluttered by neon lights. She'll cry when the police question her about your death; they'll think it's something like guilt.

*It's sad, though,* she'll say. *Don't you think it's just so sad?*

The police will say *it's sad, sure,* send her out to the waiting room with your other roommates, say *thanks for your time,* send them home. Your roommates will take a bus back to the apartment, sit together on the couch, knee-clutching, throw out your expired milk, put an ad on Craigslist for a new girl: *Quiet, clean. Won't take up much space.*

Your mother will take the bus in from the suburbs. The police will give her what is left of your things, one silver-plated earring, torn nylons, macramé bracelet that your baby sister made.

*She never took that off,* your mother will tell them, packing it with your other things from the police in a plastic shopping bag. Your roommates will give her the rest from the apartment, packed in your ripped-side suitcase, except your nicest dress, which the Wyoming girl will tuck among her own clothes for safekeeping.

*She was a good girl,* she'll say to your mother.

*She was a lot of things,* your mother will say. *I don't know about good.*

Your mother will take your things back home on the bus; you'll go back home casketed broken-doll in the back of a mortuary van.

The Wyoming girl will wear your nicest dress to an audition the day of your funeral. She won't know it's the day of your funeral; your family will keep it quiet so the press won't come. Only one local reporter will be there, tall and too thin, all knees and nose, write a first-person account on *the death of a flower, the funeral of a flower.*

The Wyoming girl will tell the casting director *this dress belongs to a dead girl.* The casting director will find that interesting, find her memorable, say: *you've got the role.* She'll be cast as Dead Girl #2 in a popular serial drama about a detective who doesn't play by the rules. A detective in a trench coat, a detective with a past. A detective who always gets his man.

The Wyoming girl will practice lying still on the floor of the apartment.

*How do I look?* she'll say to your other roommates. *Do I look like a real dead girl?*

They'll say: *Yes. Yes, you look like a real dead girl.*

The Wyoming girl and your other roommates will stream your last movie on their phones when it's released, call it *your* movie, though it never belonged to you, though nothing ever did. They'll pause and start, pause and start, shift through frame by frame. This could be your knee, this could be the back of your head, the way that one stands, she could be you.

*There,* they'll say, and point at the screens, *there, there, that must be her,* but they'll never be quite sure if they're right.

# Being the Murdered Politician

The thing about being the murdered politician is you set the plot in motion.

You will be speaking, you will be *orating*, you will be so vividly alive, everyone will remember that, everyone will say.

*She was so alive.*

You will be speaking, you will be standing behind the podium and then falling backward, a bloom of blood under your clutching hand. Everyone will be ducking or screaming or turning their heads to see, everyone will say *it was just like on television, I didn't think it would be like that, it didn't feel real.*

Your campaign advisor will perform CPR, your advisor will shout *is anyone a doctor,* and people will say *that's just like television too,* will say that the whole thing seemed so *phony*, and there will be videos of your death, videos that get reported and pulled and released again, the widening of your eyes, the sharpness of your last breath.

*That can't be real,* people will say, click the play button again, again.

Your campaign advisor will find the videos when she googles your name. She will report them every time, she will throw out the outfit she was wearing the day you died, expensive jacket, sensible shoes. She will drop them in the garbage near your campaign headquarters, cover them with *Vote For* posters, stickers of your face.

She will speak to the media: *We have to keep trying, for her.*

She'll say: *Please vote.*

Your campaign advisor will start sleeping on the couch in your headquarters, your advisor will shake hands with the volunteers, the interns, as they leave, thank them, profusely, for their time.

*It just doesn't seem real,* they'll say, hold onto her hand a beat too long. *None of it seems real.*

Your campaign advisor will nod, will throw out more and more of your campaign things, will forget to wash her hair for a week. She'll sit at your computer, the password your name and the election year, anyone could have hacked you, she always used to say, and shake her head when you laughed, said *but who would want to?*

She'll miss the sound of your laughter the most. The gleam of your white teeth second, the way you were so hopeful, the way you thought things could be changed yet, changed still. Your hands enveloping hers every night before you went home, the way you'd say *thank you* then, like you meant it. The way you said, when you first saw your campaign headquarters, the shake of your head: *Oh, I can hardly believe it. It doesn't seem real.*

And the videos will pop up, again, again, again, the crack of the rifle, the hush of your body hitting the ground, the quiet release of balloons by an intern mistaking their cue, rising up into the sky, red, white, blue balloons peppering the air, and then gone, gone, gone.

# Being the Murdered Mama

The thing about being the murdered mama is that you set the plot in motion.

Before you were killed, your friends gave you knit blankets, onesies, little rubber pacifiers. Called you *little mama,* said *You're so round you look like you've got a basketball under your shirt.*

*Little mama,* they said, *what are you going to name the baby?*

Your baby will be given a name you don't choose. Your baby will be pulled from you like straggle cornflower clutching earth; your baby will be swaddled and fed, tucked into a secondhand bassinet.

Your baby will be given a name and so will you, for several days, *Jane Doe*, until you are identified, until you are given back to your family, unstitched, torn.

The newspapers will love photos of you, your too-serious mouth, unplucked eyebrows, tangle of hair at the base of your neck.

The newspapers will ask has anyone seen your baby, the newspapers will shed crocodile tears for your young life.

*Just a kid herself,* they'll say.

The newspapers will have photos of you and photos of you to choose from, until they finally pick the one they like best, how you're almost smiling, how your eyes are open too wide, how the crooked of your one-time-broken nose is charming. The newspapers will run this photo with their articles about you and your missing baby.

Your face will be on the nightly news, your face will be clickbait, irresistible.

People will say: *that poor thing*, will say: *what a dangerous world we live in.*

They'll say: *What about her baby?*

Your baby will be found, within the week, in its secondhand bassinet, in an apartment that isn't yours, that still holds the scent, somehow, of your shampoo.

Your parents will be given care of your baby; your parents will change its name. Your parents will say: *Please, let us have our privacy.*

And your face will slowly disappear, except at your parents' house, where your mother will pull photos out of old albums, have them framed and placed all over the house, take your baby round to them every day, *this is your mama, this is your mama, this is your mama.*

Your baby's first word will be *mama,* formula-mouthed, grasping-fingered, *mama, mama.* Your baby will be sitting up on its own when the trial begins, when your face is back in all the newspapers, that same wide-eyed, almost-smiling photograph.

People will see your face and think they know you from somewhere, *didn't she used to be somebody,* will have forgotten how they knew you before, how they wept before, for your tragedy.

*What a dangerous world,* they'll say.

The trial will be televised. Your baby and your parents will stay locked up in their home, except for when your mother sends your father out for groceries. He'll linger in the baby aisle at the box store, remember feeding you pureed carrots with a tiny spoon, remember you once gave him a chain of paper clips, red and white, red and white, like a candy cane, to decorate his office at Christmastime, your small hands dropping the paper-clip chain into his own, *here, papa, here.* Your father will pick out a box of oatmeal and a can of peas before leaning over the grocery cart and crying your name, again, again, again, until the store supervisor has to escort him back to his car, gripping his shoulder. Your father will clutch the oatmeal and the peas in his shaking hands. Your father will hold them like nothing else.

Your mother and your baby will be waiting at home. Your mother will turn on the television, baby in her lap. She'll see the face of your killer, done up in plain, flattering makeup, her hands folded in her lap. *Desperate to be a mother* is how she'll be portrayed. Your mother's breath will hitch and catch, hitch and catch. Your mother will see your face when the news stations flash it on the screen, and your baby will see too, say *mama* the way it's been taught, *mama, mama,* and your mother will say *yes,* say *yes, that's your mama,* hold your baby against her chest, the way, she'll remember, she used to hold you.

# Being the Murdered Mermaid

The thing about being the murdered mermaid is you set the plot in motion.

The other mermaids will refuse to work until the tank you were found in is replaced; the other mermaids will sit in the back room of the bar, sew aquamarine sequins onto the tails of their costumes. The oldest mermaid will be bad at sewing, will jab her fingertip, jab her fingertip, jab her fingertip, wince every time. The other mermaids will pretend not to see; the other mermaids will do her the favor of not letting her ask for help.

The back room of the bar will be quiet, except when one of the bartenders opens the door, the sound of Piano Peggy, 87 years old, never missed a night, seeping in. The oldest mermaid will get a little teary-eyed when she hears the Moonlight Sonata, no kind of a song for a bar, say: *Oh, I jabbed my finger again, that's all.*

The mermaids will sew quietly in the back room, stare quietly when the door is opened. All the mermaids will have green eyes like you did, all the mermaids will be able to hold their breath for two minutes, three, four, five. They'll keep in practice in the back room while the tank is being drained, colorful fish they swim with stowed safely in various aquariums throughout the bar. They'll watch for the nod of the oldest mermaid, *now,* suck in their breath, hold, hold, hold.

For the mermaids, it will seem like everything has gone underwater since you died. The hush and quiet of the sea. They'll like to think of their time in the tank as being part of the sea, the tickle of fish fin brushing against their shoulders, winks of the patrons blurred by hazy water.

The mermaids will say it's good they're getting this chance to repair their costumes, it never seemed like there was time before, and the door will come open and Piano Peggy will be playing Chopin's Raindrop Prelude, music hanging heavy in the air.

*I jabbed my finger again,* the oldest mermaid will say, and the other mermaids will dip their heads and nod, think of the honky-tonk Piano Peggy used to play before you were killed, how sometimes you would slip some of your tip money into her jar on slow nights. You always thought Piano Peggy never saw, but she could tell by the damp of dollar bill, a different kind than beer or whiskey, smile, throw in a little Joplin ragtime, and you'd waggle in your mermaid tail, like you were nearly dancing.

Manager Joe will check in on the mermaids from time to time. He'll be thick and sturdy, and they will think of manatees when they see him, will long for the taste of saltwater when he says to them from the doorway, *soon, girls, soon.*

Manager Joe won't say you were his favorite, but everyone will know you were. You were everyone's favorite, *the best,* they'll say, *the best mermaid,* gaze at the lowering water in the tank, toast you with blue mermaid cocktails, teal umbrellas tipped sadly to the side.

Manager Joe will donate money to your family so they can afford to take you to the sea and scatter your ashes there.

*She always wanted to visit the ocean,* Manager Joe will say, put a folded-up check in your mother's hand.

The other mermaids will think Manager Joe wouldn't pay their parents to take them to the sea, the other mermaids will think they'll outlive Manager Joe anyway, the way he wheezes sometimes, like a fish twisting on land.

The other mermaids will sew, sew, sew.

When the bar goes dark for the night, the mermaids will come out of the back room, sequins and costumes stowed in bags tucked over their shoulders. The mermaids won't speak to each other as they leave, except the way they have talked through the tank, whisper of eyelash flutter, twist and curve of hand. The other mermaids will know, when the oldest mermaid stumbles over a gesture, sore fingertip tripping, will blink and curl their fingers, reply without words: *yes, yes, we miss her too.*

# Being the Murdered Daughter

The thing about being the murdered daughter is you set the plot in motion.

Your father will make the calls while your mother weeps on the couch. Your mother will say to him *you always were the strong one,* will pour him a glass of wine, will pull the phone from his hand.

*Not now,* she'll say, *not now,* into the receiver, hang up on her sister-in-law, who will be clutching her own phone in her hand, who will be thinking how small you were when you were born.

*Not now,* your mother will say again, put her arms around your tall father, go up on her toes like she has always done when she wanted a kiss.

Your house will become full after your death, aunts and uncles and cousins sleeping on the couch, on the floor, looking in through the gap of your cracked bedroom door, the rose and lavender of your bedspread, blush of your walls. Your littlest cousin will keep toddling in, your littlest cousin will cry every time he is picked up and pulled away, chubby little hands reaching and reaching. Something in his shrieking will make your mother think of daybreak, peek of sun at rise. Roosters, maybe, she'll think. She'll think there is quiet beneath all the noise, always quiet.

Your mother and your father will be alone in this full house, will eat half-bites of neighbors' casseroles, lay their forks crooked on still-full plates; will cover their ears at the moments of silence in the house, to hear the rumble of their own bodies; will have the television on in the middle of the night, muted glow filling their eyes.

Your mother will play the classic movie channel, will fall in love with the crease of Greta Garbo's forehead when she scowls, will say *doesn't Garbo resemble her?* touch the screen with the flat of her hand, *something in the eyebrows, I think.*

Your mother and your father will float in the noise of your full house, in the sound of footsteps, voices, whisper-breath. Your mother will feel like she is leaving her body when she lies flat on her bed in the night, won't be able to feel your father beside her, the cool of the sheet, creak of old mattress. The house will fall quiet except for the small snores from cousins' mouths, the curl and uncurl of restless legs. Your mother will hear, in the hush of the night house, a sound from the attic like the rustling of stiff skirts, touch your father's shoulder.

He'll say: *I hear it too.*

Together in the dark, your parents will go through the house to the attic entrance. The breathing of cousins will be like receding waves.

Your mother will think how different the house is at night, how different everything is at night, will stop in the kitchen, look out the window at the flat sky, at the distant lights of town.

*It's always waiting, isn't it,* she'll say to your father, touch his shoulder again, *to be quiet.*

*What's always waiting?*

She'll say: *Everything.*

The entrance to the attic is in the garage; you never went there when you were alive, up the pull-down ladder, into that dark place where your parents stored all the things that thought they might use someday again; only your father went that you ever saw.

Both your parents will go this time, turning on the garage light to find the hanging ladder cord, stirring your father's oldest sister briefly awake, and she will think again of the smallness of you as a baby, the crinkle of your fingers and toes. In the morning, she won't remember waking, will think she had dreamed of you, will think *it was all only a dream.*

Your father will climb the ladder first, then your mother. They will be looking for your ghost there; they will push past stacks of encyclopedias, empty shoeboxes, pretty wine bottles, inhale the scent of ancient Christmas mittens. They will hold hands, they will breathe together, they will sigh dry tears when your mother opens the attic window and the small grey bats that have been nesting in the attic startle and stretch, and rush out, rush out into the night.

# Being the Murdered Muse

The thing about being the murdered muse is you set the plot in motion.

You'll be found in the sculptor's studio. You had a spare key, you were always letting yourself in, the sculptor will tell the police. He'll dial emergency from his cell when he sees you there, clutching one of his patrons by the arm, *oh, hello,* he'll say to the operator, voice tremoring, *oh hello.*

The sculptor will cover you with a shroud from one of his sculptures before the police arrive. He'll say *I know I shouldn't have done it, but she seemed so defenseless like that, so weak.*

He'll say: *She was my inspiration, you know.*

The sculptor will have a habit of moving his hands when he talks, like he is carving the curve of your body into the air. He'll never finish his last sculpture of you, leave you alabaster, leave you ghost-pale and perfect, his patrons will say, *perfect.* The way people like to think of women like you, disarmed Venus, cream Aphrodite.

The sculptor used to tell you the whiteness of the old Greek statues was just an accident of time, that they were originally colorful and bright.

*Garish,* he said, and winked, touched you in a clinical, measuring way.

*I found her,* he'll tell his patrons, tell the police, tell the interviewers who ask. *She was this beautiful, beautiful creature, and no one else saw.*

He will go to his studio, he will walk the outline of where your body lay, walk in a stiff, rote way. His hands will be twitching like birds falling out of the sky.

*I must,* he will say to the patron who has been at his side since you were found, *create.*

He will sculpt you over and over again; you will become clearer with each statue he creates, but it will always be the unfinished one that he comes back to, that he *loves.* He'll say *she's perfect like this, isn't she, undone and perfect,* touch the curve of a pale elbow that is both yours and not yours with more care than he ever showed for your skin.

He will take a hammer to the other statues, crack them, knock holes into them, think *she is dying again,* think *I am killing her again,* knock off a nose, fingers and toes, crush the pieces under his soles. There will be dust floating in the air, dust and dust and dust; he will think *I am breathing in pieces of her.*

The sculptor will host an exhibition in your honor, he'll say *in your honor*, populate it with his failed sculptures of you, name them with Roman numerals, II, III, IV, say *it is so hard, you know, to capture a soul once it is lost.*

Your unfinished sculpture will be the centerpiece of the show, Roman Numberal I, will be *oohed* over, will be *aahed.* His patrons will admire it between glasses of rosé, touch the coldness of it with the light tips of their hands, compare it to the flutter of a butterfly wing, the scent of a particular flower: *it's not her, but it is, oh, it is.*

*Oh, yes,* the sculptor will say, raise his glass heavenward, tip it in toast toward the statue of you. *Yes, it is.*

# Being the Murdered Chanteuse

The thing about being the murdered chanteuse is you set the plot in motion.

They'll set up a shrine for you near the piano; you always touched the piano when you sang, ran fingertip along its wood, leaned against it backwards, bent over it, stretched both arms long, curled song out of your throat whiskey-voiced. They'll put a photograph of you on a table, surround it with white tapered candles.

The candles will burn down to nubs. The patrons will tap their knuckles against the table, thumb-touch the wooden frame of your photograph, remember the sound of your voice, *how it soared,* they'll say.

Before you were killed, the pianist was half in love with you. He'd say *half,* like love was a thing that could be measured, portioned out, buy you shots of apple brandy, liked the way you stuck your pinky out when you drank — *such a fine lady*, he always said, and laughed, laughed.

He'll wear the same tux he has always worn. He'll play the same songs. He'll run scales and arpeggios when the nightclub is first coming open for the night, chairs being unstacked from tabletops, glasses being laid out at the bar. He'll do the things he's always done, except he too will touch the flat of table, run thumb over photo frame. He'll like your eyes in the photograph, how they look wild, how they look wounded.

The staff will come in bit by bit for the night, séance-rap your shrine table, touch edge of photo frame. They'll think it feels different in the nightclub now, a kind of heavy in the air, like they are always inhaling smoke or fog. They'll take the chairs down from the tabletops, scrape the legs across the floor, listen to the broken-chord song of the pianist warming up. The bartender will pour a shot of apple brandy, set it on top of the piano. It will sit there all night. It will always sit there all night.

The bartender will remember how you'd always take a whiskey with lemon at the end of your shift, lemon for your throat, whiskey *for the hell of it*, throw it back, throw it down.

The bartender will remember how you used to smile. He'll tap his knuckles against your table, they'll be calling it *your table* now, little round teetering thing, covered in candle wax. He'll tap his knuckles there, brush thumb over the frame of your photograph, remember how once your hand brushed his when you took your whiskey with lemon, how he tried to make the touch linger, the thin and taper of your fingers.

The nightclub will open, the chairs will come down.

The patrons will sit at their tables, listen to the new girl. She'll wear black satin like you, gloves that come up over her elbows like you. The waitresses will show her your eye makeup trick, bit of concealer along your lid, that will make her eyes pop like yours, that will make her seem like you, all eyes and voice and the slick of satin.

*She's good,* the patrons will say. *She's very good.*

They'll pretend they aren't comparing her to you, aren't finding her lacking. They'll leave her tips in the jar on the piano, they'll tap your table, touch the photo frame.

The new girl will do it too, tap-touch, tap-touch, every night. The new girl will, and everybody. They'll think sometimes *have we always done this? When did we start doing this?* They'll barely remember to look at your face in the photograph, touch the frame perfunctorily, knuckle-tap the table. From time to time, they'll replace the candles at your shrine and light them, watch the smoke wind into the air, think *how it soared,* how your voice soared.

# Being the Murdered Cheerleader

The thing about being the murdered cheerleader is you set the plot in motion.

The marching band will spell out your name at the next game, tubas serpentining past rows of flutes and trombones. The cheerleading squad will present your parents with a bouquet, *lilies were her favorite,* your father will say.

You were a daddy's girl, red convertible with vanity plates — *SPO1LD* — keys for Christmas, oil changes, gas card. Your mother smiled in a pinched way when your father showed you the convertible, red, cherry red, your mother kept her arms folded over her chest.

Your father will hold the lilies from the cheerleading squad and openly weep. Your mother will stand that same way beside him, arms folded, lower lip shuddering. Your mother will look out the front window of your house at that cherry red convertible in the driveway, hand trembling as she holds the drapes to one side: *We should get rid of it.*

In their sad, thin vase on the dining room table, the lilies will wilt and sag, their petals falling away. Your mother will leave the bouquet until your father says *please*, finally *please,* take it out to the garbage, drop the vase in, grimace at the shattering of glass.

Before you were murdered, the football team couldn't win a game. After your death, they will make touchdown after touchdown. They will be inspired; they will be warriors. They'll go to the state championships, dedicate the game to you. The marching band will play Cohen's *Hallelujah*; the marching band will be experts at shaping your name on the field. They could do it with their eyes closed. Some of the saxophones will. People in the stands will hold paper printout photos of you, shout, shout, shout your name.

You will be more loved than you ever were when you were alive, daddy's girl, *SPOILD*, drove too fast in your red convertible, kissed too many boys, wore skirts too short, laughed at the unpopular kids. You didn't have any friends, not real ones, you thought, that you could tell anything to, that you could trust. Just girls that wanted to wear their eyeliner like yours, girls that wanted to ride in your red convertible.

*You're my best friend,* you declared to those girls, and stole their boyfriends behind their backs. Not because you ever liked their boyfriends, but because you felt it was expected of girls like you.

The girl who lasted longest, who played stupidest, will replace you on the cheerleading squad.

*She was my best friend,* she'll say, be the one at the top of the pyramid, holding framed photo of you in both her hands. Sometimes she'll even pretend to cry.

She'll go to prom with the boyfriend she caught with you, let him hold her by her waist when the deejay plays Mazzy Star.

He'll say: *I never loved her, you know.*

She'll say: *I know,* let him take her to a hotel after, let him take her *in* a hotel after. Lie beside him on the stiff hotel bed as he sleeps, sheets tangled round her ankles, prom dress wrinkled on the floor, think: *it will never get better than this.*

She'll get a tattoo on her ankle, white lilies, so that when anyone asks, she can say: *My best friend loved lilies. They were her favorite flower.*

She'll say this until she believes it, until she forgets she ever hated you, *she was my best friend.*

At the state championship game, she'll *rah,* she'll *rah,* she'll *go team,* she'll be lifted to the top of the pyramid, holding your framed photo above her head.

She'll hold your photo, shout your name, let loose her grip on the frame, let it slip from her fingers, watch from the top of the pyramid, the falling and the falling. And when the glass shatters against the ground, she will, finally, really, cry.

# Being the Murdered Jogger

The thing about being the murdered jogger is you set the plot in motion.

They'll leave you on the side of the road. A passing motorist will stop for the purple of your scarf. He'll check for your pulse, touch your bare wrist, your half-covered throat. He'll hear the music, still, pouring from your headphones.

He'll call the police first, his boss next.

*I found someone,* he'll say. *I mean, I found a dead woman.*

The motorist will loosen his tie while he waits for the police to come; the motorist will rub his left temple. He'll wish he had something to cover you up with, wish he hadn't seen your scarf, wish he hadn't stopped.

The motorist's wife used to be a pole vaulter in college. He'll call her third, after the police, after his boss. He'll be crying by then, like he hasn't done since his father died, hiccupping, heavy tears.

*What can I do,* the former pole vaulter wife will say. *What do you want me to do?*

That evening, the former pole vaulter wife will take the motorist out for dinner. They'll have sushi and drink sake from a carafe. They won't speak to one another, just touch fingertips from time to time, gaze out onto the streetlight-lit sidewalk. The motorist will remember watching his wife pole vault in college, how it looked like she could fly.

When they get ready for bed that night, he'll say: *it must have been harder than it looked.* He'll say: *You made it look so easy, I mean.*

You'll be in the morgue while the wife kisses the motorist good night, cups his head against her shoulder, tries to shelter him from the bad dreams to come.

You'll be in the morgue, and the medical examiner will be driving in from the next town over. He'll be drinking cold coffee from a Styrofoam cup, blinking slow and slower. He'll be wishing there was better funding in the county, another medical examiner to pick up the slack. He'll nap for fifteen minutes in the holding area before security unlocks the door to the morgue.

The medical examiner will have a habit of talking to the bodies. He'll talk to you. He'll say how his kids are in college now, except the one who drowned — *he tried to rescue a girl,* he'll say. *He did, he saved her. But he drowned instead.*

He'll say: *Sometimes the universe wants balance.*

The medical examiner will like the curve of your eyes; he'll think you were probably a devoted reader. He'll imagine that you had a reading chair at home, stack of books beside it, one in your hand, a purring grey cat on your lap.

The medical examiner will be so gentle when he opens you. He'll think of his drowned son.

In the morning, there will be a news brief in the paper, a photo of your purple scarf lying sibilant on the ground. There will be tongue clucks from women who do yoga behind locked doors. There will be shaking of their heads.

*How terrible,* they'll say to their husbands. *Don't you think it's terrible?*

*It's terrible,* the husbands will agree. *It's so terrible.*

The wives will know it's not terrible for their husbands the way it is for them. The wives will button their jackets up to their chins, the wives will clutch their car keys in their hands, think they hear the sound of footsteps behind them.

The husbands will say again: *It's so terrible.*

The motorist will find your photograph in the newspaper, show it to his former pole vaulter wife while she laces her shoes.

*This is her,* he'll say. *The woman I found.*

The motorist will remember the cold of your skin when he touched you; the motorist will never be able to listen to the song he heard from your headphones again.

The former pole vaulter wife will lean in, kiss him on the side of his face.

*I'm going,* she'll say.

*Now, though? It's not light yet.*

She'll say again: *I'm going.*

He'll watch her from the front doorway, watch her as she starts to run, watch till she goes round the corner, think of how she went into the air when she was a pole vaulter, think of how she flew.

# Being the Murdered Girlfriend

The thing about being the murdered girlfriend is you set the plot in motion.

Your boyfriend will say: *I was just playing around.*

He'll say: *I didn't mean to.*

He'll say: *The gun just went off.*

His mother will wait outside when the police arrive. His mother will smoke a cigarette on the back step, look up at the sky, try not to think of your body on the floor of the family room, try not to think of the stain on the carpet. She'll say to her husband later *let's just pull it all up, God, let's burn it, I don't care, I just want it gone.* She'll smoke one cigarette, two, three. Her hands will shake.

She'll say to her son when the police say he has to come with them: *It will be all right. Everything will be all right.*

After you are buried, she'll tell her friends: *I never cared for that girl. I knew she was trouble.*

Her friends will nod. Her friends will all have sons too. Her friends will think of their sons as *precious boys*, tucked them in as children with forehead kisses and blanket-smoothing hands: *Sleep well, my precious boy.*

They will know, like mothers of sons before them, about girls like you, girls who bring good boys to ruin.

They'll see your photo in the newspaper — it will run once, the day after, clipped from the school yearbook — whisper over your heavy eye makeup, your twitch of a smile, the black shirt you wore, *low-cut,* they'll say to each other, *too low-cut.*

*Watch out for girls like this*, they'll tell their sons. *Girls like this are trouble.*

Your boyfriend's mother will hire a lawyer. The lawyer will wear nice suits, cheap ties, speak over the top of people, carry a briefcase with a combination lock.

*It was an accident,* the lawyer will say. *A tragic accident.*

He'll get your boyfriend sent home. Your boyfriend's mother will pick him up at the courthouse, take him out for hamburgers, buy him a chocolate milkshake. She'll think of how she did the same thing when he was young, after baseball games, *do you remember*, and your boyfriend will say *I do, kind of.*

He will sleep in his own bed, he will ignore the torn-up carpet, the reek of bleach. He will grow used to the scent, the way his mother and father will too, something that never quite goes, that scent, something like a ghost. When his friends come by, they'll say *what's that smell?*

Your boyfriend will say: *I don't smell anything.*

He'll say, when they ask, when anybody asks: *It was an accident.*

He'll say: *I never wanted to hurt her.*

His mother will nod, lips pressed firm. *Of course not. My son isn't that kind of boy.*

His mother will stand behind him at the sentencing, hand clutched firm on his shoulder. Later, he will show her she has left marks. In time they will fade, little fingerprint bruises disappearing and disappearing away.

She will only release her grip when the judge pronounces *negligent homicide, community service.*

She'll say: *Oh, thank you. Oh, God, thank you.*

She'll wait outside the courthouse for her son and the lawyer, smoke a cigarette while she waits, loose one in the bottom of her purse. She'll think, idly, of quitting. She'll hear the courthouse doors come open, turn to see her son come out, her precious boy, drop the half-smoked cigarette to the ground, grind it out with her heel, *my precious boy*, and your boyfriend will smile: *Mom, let's go home.*

And she won't know, and no one will, how you rode beside him in his pickup one night, how he took you backroading the dirt trails behind his house, said to you, *when you hit this rise just right, sometimes it feels like you're flying.*

And you rode in the cab beside him, *flew* beside him, looked out the window and thought how far away and small everything seemed, how it didn't seem like there was a city anymore at all, how it was you and him, alone in all the world. All you could hear was engine roar, low hum of the country station fade in and out. You looked forward and there was something there, something small, cat, maybe, or rabbit, prairie dog. And you said *oh*, felt the truck go over the top of it, didn't cry, weren't the kind of girl who would cry over a small thing like that, over a small thing that had been alive and wasn't alive anymore, but you said *oh* again, looked over at your boyfriend and saw, in the moonlight, the brilliance of his smile.

# Being the Murdered Taxidermist

The thing about being the murdered taxidermist is you set the plot in motion.

They will leave your house for days, won't find you for days, the neighborhood kids going past on their bicycles, whispering of hauntings, saying *Frankenstein, what happened to Frankenstein,* always called you that; mail piling up in your box.

The last woman you brought home will remember you had a squirrel in a miniature rocking chair reading a miniature book. She'll remember the little wire-rimmed glasses it wore the best, how they reminded her of her grandmother.

She asked: *Is this yours? I mean, did you make this?* and touched the stiff fur, wondered if it felt anything like it had when it was alive, wondered if there were such things as the ghosts of squirrels.

She will see your name on social media later, looking you up on Facebook, wondering why you hadn't called like you said. She will see your name among a list of the dead, lay her phone down on its face, wonder again about the ghosts of squirrels.

Her friends will say: *You knew her? The dead lady?*

She'll say: *A bit. I mean, we just went out the once*

She'll say: *It's not like we were friends.*

She'll tell them about your date, need to tell, need to say your name, need to say: *I knew her and now she is dead.* She'll tell them how you met up at a cramped little Asian fusion place with dirty-booth seats, flickering candle on the table, how you held your hand cupped above the flame, told her *I am holding in the warmth*, and she thought there was something charming about that.

She didn't know, she'll tell her friends, that you were a taxidermist when you met. Your profile didn't say. What she liked about you, she'll say, was your umber lipstick in your profile photo, the way you peered through your glasses at the camera like a frightened, angry thing.

*Like an animal,* she'll say. *Like she was some kind of beautiful animal.*

She'll tell her friends how she went back to your place, how you shared two bottles of plum wine at the restaurant, how the sushi chef looked up when you came in and, she will swear, winked. How you leaned over the *ebi nigiri*, said to her, *come back to my place,* how you handled your chopsticks so *deftly,* she'll tell her friends, *deftly.* How you whispered in her ear at the door to your house, *I'm a taxidermist, you know, don't be surprised,* and she thought it was just a line.

*You know?* she'll say to her friends. *Just something to make her seem interesting.*

But you turned on the light and she saw the shadow shapes in the house were really the corpses of animals — *carcasses, maybe,* she'll say, *isn't that what they call them* — posed in various ways. Some looked like regular animals, she thought, or the way she imagined regular animals would look, but there were others like the little book-reading squirrel, made to look like people.

She said: *Why?*

You said: *Doesn't it make you laugh? It makes me laugh.*

You said: *It's just death, you know?,* and kissed her in your bedroom, pulling her hand away from the squirrel's fur, laid her down on your bed, and she looked up at all the glass animal eyes as you unbuttoned her blouse, said: *I think we are being watched.*

She won't tell that part to her friends. Not about the squirrel and the glasses, or about how she took *your* glasses off while you kissed, put them on herself so that it was a different world for her there in your house, distorted, blurred, *is this what you see,* she said, but you had already closed your eyes, then, to kiss her, so you said, *I don't see anything.*

She won't tell her friend how you turned on one of the machines for her when she asked, sitting naked on the edge of your bed, rumble like a lawnmower, she said *what is that,* and you said, *a fleshing machine* and the way you smiled made her smile too, *a fleshing machine,* she said, and watched you touch the tip of your finger to a bear's roaring teeth. She was slow in putting her clothing back on, and slow in taking your hand and following you, through the rows of posed animals, through the smell of sawdust, back into the world outside.

And when you are found, days after she has gone, days after you promised *I'll call, I will, I like you,* days after you deleted her number from your phone, you are found by two of the children on their bicycles, daring each other inside. They will whisper *wolves,* they will whisper *bears,* they will see a skull on your workbench and be awed by the size of its jaw, the white of its mouth, they will think dinosaur, they will think monster, they will think *Frankenstein,* and they will find you, there in your house, just one more animal amongst the others.

# Being the Murdered Roommate

The thing about being the murdered roommate is you set the plot in motion.

There will be sightings of you after you are gone, girl with hair cut like yours, girl with mauve lipstick, girl in a cardigan like the one you always wore. Your friends will think they are seeing a ghost, your friends will be haunted, following the shade of you past storefronts and around corners, seeing your face gazing out the window of a bus.

They will call your name and the girl who resembles you will turn her head, begin to turn, will be swallowed up in the crowd, will disappear.

Your parents will go to your apartment to collect your things, your parents will bring empty boxes and bags, leave the trunk open, car slantwise on the street. Your mother will open your bedroom window despite an early spring chill, she will press her face against the screen like she used to do as a child, look out onto the street, see the shadow of your footstep in the sidewalk, hear the winding wraith of your laugh.

Your roommate will be gone when your parents go to your apartment, leave a note pinned to the door: *I thought you would want to be alone.* Your parents will think there is something familiar about her handwriting, will wonder between themselves about the roommate they have never met, the hush and pause of her voice on the phone when they told her they'd be coming for your things: *oh, of course.*

Your mother will go through your jewelry box, pluck things out bit by bit, drop them back in, the clatter of costume jewelry, falling through her fingers like lost raindrops.

*I can't find her favorite earrings,* your mother will say. *They're not anywhere.*

*She must have,* your father will say, staring at the walls and not seeing, staring at the rectangle places where posters you had hung have been torn down, *been wearing them.*

He'll say: *When it happened, she must have been wearing them.*

*Of course,* your mother will say, *of course, that must be it,* snap the lid shut on the jewelry box, run her hand over the top of it. They will carry your things down the wooden stairs that sing with each step, down and down and down, shut them up in the trunk, look up at the open window of your apartment, feel like there is something they are missing, something they have forgotten.

*There must be something else,* your mother will say, even as they are driving away, and your father will adjust the rearview mirror and see, for a moment, your ghost, slipping up the concrete step to your apartment building.

He'll tell your mother later, when they have gotten home, when they have laid the boxes and bags of your things in your old bedroom, when your mother sits on your bed with Mr. Floppy your grey stuffed bunny pressed to her chest, seeking the smell of you in his worn, long ears.

He'll tell your mother: *I thought I saw her ghost.*

*I see her everywhere too,* your mother will say.

And they will sit together on your bed with Mr. Floppy, and your father will say *maybe it is just a part of her we are still holding onto,* and your mother's knuckles will go white with clutching and she will stare up at the ceiling of your old bedroom and release a sound from her throat that begins as a groan, ends as a wail, and they will sit and not touch, in the shatter of quiet between them.

And at your old apartment, your roommate will blot the mauve lipstick from her mouth, take the earrings from her ears, lay them on the bathroom counter, gaze into the mirror, admire the cut and sway of her hair, whisper *twins, don't you think we could have been twins.*

# Being the Murdered Classmate

The thing about being the murdered classmate is you set the plot in motion.

You were killed by a monster, they'll say. You were killed by the hollow man.

The other kids will draw pictures of the hollow man. He will be all mouth and teeth and gnarled reaching hands. They will draw in him stolen classroom chalk on the playground concrete, in the backs of math books in pencil, on the tops of their desks with black pen, in tabletop dust at home.

*What are you drawing?* their parents will say.

*A bad man,* the other kids will answer. *The bad man.*

At school, they will whisper of the hollow man. Jenise from Class 5-B will have seen him cross through the alley behind her house the night of a thunderstorm, flare of lightning illuminating him through the thin fingers of trees. Derrick from

6-A will say the hollow man was peeping in his basement window, looking in at the baby in its crib, and his twin sister Delphine will say she looked out the car window on the way home from ballet and saw him loping down the sidewalk.

She'll say: *Like a wolf.*

She'll say: *Just like a wolf.*

The parents will shake their heads, the parents will say *there is no such thing as the hollow man,* the parents will twist the knobs on the door at night, will say, *see, you see? It's locked.*

*It's locked, you're safe.*

The other kids won't say, but they will know, they will know that there are things that can get through locked doors, that there is badness all around.

The other kids will try to conjure your ghost on the playground, with the shiniest pebbles and torn strips of paper from your old notebook and their hands that all touched your desk after the bell rang for recess, as they lined up to leave, one hand, another, another, touch, touch, touch.

They'll spread the paper strips in a circle under their feet to keep them from fluttering away, the swirl of your handwriting air-light beneath their shoes; they'll hold hands in a circle; they'll place the pebbles in their mouths; they'll say, tongue-heavy, *are you there, are you there?*

*Tell us,* they'll say. *Tell us about the hollow man.*

They'll wait and call, wait and call, till the recess aide comes over, says *what are you kids doing,* and Scarlett from 4-A choke-swallows her pebble and begins to cry.

And when they come back, your desk will be moved from its space, pressed against the back wall like when Jeromy got in trouble for pinching all the girls on the back to see if they were wearing bras yet, your desk will be like something punished, your desk will be a haunted shrine.

Your desk will stay there for the rest of the school year, the teacher's eyes going to it, sometimes, during science lessons, the teacher remembering how she was the one had to tell them, when it happened, *your friend,* she said, *your friend is dead,* and one of them said *was it the hollow man?*, and then another said, and then another, *no, nothing like that*, she protested, and then some of them had, finally, cried. The teacher will look at your desk, again, again, again, see the flutter and rustle of some dark thing, blink it away, slow.

The other kids will catch her looking, the other kids will say *teacher, what is it? What is it, teacher?*

And the teacher will rub her right eye with the back of her hand, like someone just waking, and she'll say, *nothing, it's nothing*, and she will pretend not to hear when the whispers begin, again, about the hollow man.

# Being the Murdered Hermit

The thing about being the murdered hermit is you set the plot in motion.

Your killers will gather every year on the anniversary of your death, pack bags, kiss parents goodbye, rushed, blown kisses, *we'll be good*. There will be five of them: two couples of boy and girl and the odd one out, the kid sister, the tagalong.

They will meet at the cabin in the woods. One of them will have parents who can afford things like that, cabins in the woods with wooden deck swing and barrel hot tub. They will lay their bags in the usual places, say the usual things, *has it already been a year*. They will make the trek to the place they buried you, check that the cross they fashioned out of branches and twine is still straight, will say *it looks more crooked than last year, do you think it looks more crooked?*

There will be the hushed recriminations — *you're the one that hit her* to the boy who was driving, *you're the one that said we should bury her* to the girl who did — the soft flirtation between one of the girls and the boy who is not her partner, their breaths quickening and matching pace when they stand together. The five of them will stand at your grave, bow their heads the way they have seen mourners on television shows do.

They will say *it was so dark that night,* they will say *where was the moon that night?*

They will hardly seem to change after your death, except perhaps they will whisper more, perhaps they will drive slower on dark nights, look in crowds for faces that resemble yours, wake from dreams they can barely remember, think of the lightness of your body.

Only the kid sister will change in a noticeable way, tagging along after the other four as she has always done. She will take to wearing gothic chokers and velvets, black her eyes with liner. She will read tarot fortunes, will always, always pull Death.

They will go back to the cabin where they had been staying when they killed you, they will remember how the car shuddered when it hit your body, how little damage you left, how it was almost like nothing had happened at all. They will think *maybe nothing happened at all*, but there, always, is your grave. They will remember how they dug at the ground with their bare hands, how there was dirt under their fingernails that didn't seem like it would ever come out, how they dug and dug, *deep, it has to be deep.*

They will stand at the grave they have made for you, they will drink bottled beer in your honor, they'll say *in your honor*, toast you to the sky, except the kid sister, who won't drink at all. She'll kneel beside your grave, dirtying her knees the same as she did *that night,* she will always think of it as *that night*, she will put her hand into the dirt, say *doesn't it seem like the soil has been disturbed*, and the others will laugh, say *you're just trying to scare us.* She will shuffle and shuffle her tarot deck back at the cabin, tell the others, *watch, every time* and pull Death, turn it over and over in her hands.

*Death,* she'll say, *always death.*

And the Death card will be face up on the table when the moon disappears behind the clouds and the power fails, when there is a sound like a howling, when there is something like a knocking at the door, and they will think, *oh, she has come. She has come for us at last.*

# Being the Murdered Witch

The thing about being the murdered witch is you set the plot in motion.

They will call you by things not your name, they will never know your name, never know the way you walked the length of your house every morning at the coming of light, back and forth, back and forth, hands twitching, murmuring quietly, *spells,* they would say if they had seen you, or songs. They will call you *crone,* call you *hag,* will whisper *baba yaga* behind closed fists.

*Wicked,* they will call you. *Wicked, wicked, wicked.*

They'll speak of familiars, black arched-back cats, wide-winged bats, their dip and soar, dip and soar, wart-spotted toads, *croak, croak.* They will say you had brought a plague of shiny-tailed rats upon their houses, they will say you snatched children from their beds, drank from pinpricks of their blood before putting them back. They will say they saw you dance on full-moon nights, out in the open field, *where anyone could see*, they will say, and say again, *wicked, wicked, wicked.*

They will come out onto the street after you are gone, they will come out of their squat homes, whispering to one another, mouth to ear, mouth to ear, whisper *she is gone, she is gone.*

Out onto the street with wooden matches, wax-drip candles, flick of flint, snap of spark. Their little feet will barely be able to keep from dancing; some of the children will take hold of each other's hands, spin and spin. Their laughter will drift like cotton-burst into the sky.

*She is gone,* they will say, *oh, she is gone.*

They will go flame-lit to your house where it stands, they will never know the scent of herbs in packets by your stove, the scratch of broom across dusty floor, the lay of your shoes at your bedside. They will never know the inside of your house, never dare open the door, bend to your house, bow, with their candles and matches, they will whisper, they will sing.

They will pull nothing from your house, save no books, no wood-backed chairs, none of the letters you never sent home to your mother, tucked under the pillow of your bed, the rustle of unsaid words taking you into sleep. They will stand and watch the flame lick and burn, they will sing, they will pray, *gone, she is gone,* and in the morning, when the burning is done, they will sift through the ashes of the place that had been your home, looking, looking, looking for bones.

# Being the Murdered Blonde

The thing about being the murdered blonde is you set the plot in motion.

You will be beautiful and dead. You will be famous and dead, perfect and dead.

All the girls will know your face from the photos in the paper, videos on their computer screens. They'll know the tip of your earlobe, button of your nose, cloudless sky of your eyes, porcelain of your skin. You will be perfect like the dolls they played with when they were young: blue-glass-eyed dolls with little pouting mouths that said *Mama*, stiff-legged fashion dolls that they put in stylish little outfits and plastic matching shoes, that they smashed against the boy dolls, plastic face to plastic face, pulled them apart, smashed them back together, said *this is love, this is love, this is love.*

The girls will look in their mirrors, in their reflective phone screens, dream of seeing your face there instead of their own, dream of your bloodless mouth, your ghost-pale skin when they found you. How you were bone-China thin, how the coroner must have held your hand like you were a living thing, how, they will dream, he wept.

Their parents will say: *Such a pretty girl.*

Their parents will say: *What a shame.*

And the girls will know that it's true, that it is a shame for a pretty girl to die, and also that there is something like shame in being pretty like that, boxed-and-shelved pretty, something like shame in being desired, in being wanted, in being dead.

The girls will admire how straight and white your teeth are in the photos, the pink of your tongue hidden behind them. They will wish the videos of you weren't all silent, wish for the gift of your voice. They will imagine it husky and soft, your every sentence imparted like some delicious secret.

They will love you, more than their parents do, more than, they will think, their parents love anything.

They will think: *I will never love again.*

They will think: *Not like this.*

They will love you more than the posters of smooth-faced boy bands on their bedroom walls; more than Jacob in orchestra and his dark eyelashes, the way his back arched when he played the *Scheherazade* solo at the spring concert; more than

Mr. Hammond the just-out-of-college biology teacher and his red car with all the windows down, the whip of wind in his thick hair.

This, they will think, is real love.

The girls who can will style their hair like yours, will wear clothes like yours. The neighborhood boutique will run out of crystals on a thin chain like you used to wear, the lucky girls who got one nestling them against the soft of their throats, running their fingers along twisting chain, gazing half-close-eyed out the classroom window, thinking *mine, mine, mine.*

The other girls will envy, will love, will lie: *Oh, you look just like her*, all smiles, all crystal-reaching fingertips, *can I touch, can I touch.*

*Just be careful*, the girls in necklaces will say, jutting their bird-thin throats out daringly, *be oh so careful.*

And the whisper of someone's hands against their skin, and the cool of the crystal, and they will think, like the poet said, you were never loved for yourself alone, and, when it is brightest, all the girls will sit in the sun and pray and pray for the fading of their dark hair.

# Being the Murdered Realtor

The thing about being the murdered realtor is you set the plot in motion.

The young couple will arrive early for the tour of the house. They liked the look of the hardwood floors in the photographs, and the wife will always remember, after, the sound of her heels clacking across them. They'll see your car at the curb, idling still, they'll say later *we thought that was strange, of course*, but at the time, they'll assume you are simply waiting inside.

The young couple selected you for your bus bench campaign, your smiling face beside the company logo, *Your Trust is Earned*, the young wife liked the strand of pearls around your neck, *clearly glass,* she told her husband, *glass pearl*. They liked that your voice was husky when they called to set the appointment, *whiskey voice*, the young husband said, and they imagined you smoking thin cigarettes as you drove from showing to showing, flicking the ashes out the window.

You will be on the kitchen floor when they come inside, calling *hello, hello*, and the young wife's heels will clack-clack-clack on the hardwood floor.

Later, they'll say the house already felt haunted. They'll say they could sense your presence.

*It was like she was calling out to us*, the young wife will say.

She will be the one who finds you, reach out to touch your shoulder like you are only just resting, there on the kitchen floor, say *are you all right, please say that you're all right*.

The young wife will be the one to say, years later, after the divorce, *it felt like we were cursed then. Like nothing would ever be right for us.*

The young wife will say she could never see that house again without thinking of you in it and the police with all their questions, and they brought her a cup of coffee as she stood on the sidewalk and she didn't know where it had come from, held it without drinking till it went cold, watched the steam curl into the morning air, thought of hauntings, thought of ghosts.

After that, the young couple will buy a house on the other side of town, the young couple will discuss the possibility of children. The young wife will reach for her husband in the night and remember the coldness of your skin under her hand, flinch away.

*What,* he'll say, *what?*

She'll say: *It's nothing.*

She'll say: *I'm sorry.*

The house will be cleaned up, crime scene tape pulled down, scrubbed, fumigated, put back on the market.

*It's a nice house,* the neighbors will say. *Nice people lived there.*

They won't call it the murder house, though everyone else will, driving down the street under half-moon night sky, *the murder house,* dim their headlights, turn down their stereos for the shiver-thrill running through their bodies.

The house will stay empty, except for your ghost, the young wife will tell her yoga friends, *when I touched her, there was a presence, like a puff of smoke, like a whisper of winter breath.* She'll say *I remember how cold it was, how sad.*

The house will stay empty and fall into disrepair, the neighbors will stop taking turns mowing the lawn, will stop answering calls from unknown numbers, *the murder house,* those callers, always breathily asking *tell me about the murder house.* The neighbors will be asked about you, but they will say they only knew the previous owners, *nice folks, two kids, a boy and a girl, they moved to Wisconsin, we think, they used to come to neighborhood barbecues, the wife always brought a strawberry pretzel salad.*

They didn't know you, they'll say, your business cards tucked into the backs of their wallets, magneted on refrigerator fronts, your bus bench photo fading and fading away. They never knew *you*.

# Being the Murdered Hairdresser

The thing about being the murdered hairdresser is you set the plot in motion.

The old women will say you were their favorite. The old women will say you knew how to set a permanent just right. They'll be able to point to the photographs of your children tucked into the corner edges of the mirror at your station, call them by name, ask your coworkers *how is the littlest handling it?*

The old women will like how you never tried to talk them into dye or fancy cuts, they will like how you kept things simple. They'll call you a simple girl.

*What she needed,* they'll say, *was a simple man.*

They'll all disapprove of your new boyfriend. They'll always call him your new boyfriend, even after your death, even though he had been your boyfriend for years by then, even though the littlest was his.

The old women will sniff and twitch and avert their eyes when he comes in to take your things from your station, peeling each one of the photographs delicately, they'll whisper to each other *do you think he will keep them or throw them away*, and when he leaves with your things in a box, they'll shake their heads and say, *she deserved a simple man.*

They'll say: *She deserved a better man.*

The salon will be closed the day of your service. The old women won't like that, hoping for a touchup before they head to the mortuary. They will sit in one row, shoulder to shoulder, in the mortuary chapel, their hair will be flossy as cotton candy and they will all wear the same perfume, something that hints of gardenias and white tea.

They will see your littlest come in carried by a grandfather, clutching a ragged teddy bear, and they will murmur, *how brave, such a brave child.* They will introduce themselves to your sisters, they will shake hands in that way some old women do, their own hands surrounding the other, *she was a simple girl, she was a good girl.*

After the service, they will meet for coffee at their favorite place. They will crowd around two tables, they will sit Thelma, the oldest, at the crack between them. Thelma, when she sets her coffee down after brief sips, will switch it from one table to the other.

*Do make up your mind, dear,* the others will tell her, but Thelma won't, switch her cup from one table to the other, listen and nod, listen and nod.

The old women will exchange pointed theories of your murder. It was the new boyfriend, it was an old boyfriend, it was a robbery, it was a mistake. They will think, in ways they will never admit, that somehow you deserved it, that people don't get killed that don't deserve it, that somehow, somehow, you had done bad, you had done *wrong.*

They'll say: *I wonder how the littlest is holding up.* They'll sip their coffees, they'll cluck at Thelma.

In the days after your death, they'll go back to the salon. They'll ask for Jessalyn or Brandie, they'll stare disapprovingly at their reflection in the unfamiliar mirrors, fluff their teased hair with the palms of their hands. They'll say, *no, no, not like this.*

They'll say: *She would have never done it like this.*

# Being the Murdered Lepidopterist

The thing about being the murdered lepidopterist is you set the plot in motion.

Your lover will come to your house to find you, your lover will open the door with the copy of your key you gave her, your lover will step into a kaleidoscope storm, tornado of butterfly wings. She will be crying before she has even found your body.

*I knew,* she'll say. *The butterflies would never have been loose if it had been anything else.*

She'll wipe her eyes with the cheap tissue one of the detectives gave her. *She always took such good care of them.*

*I knew,* she'll say. *I knew, I knew, I knew.*

There will be the usual investigation, there will be the memorial service and your mother embracing your lover, *you made her so happy, you know?* There will be the news articles, dwindling in size and getting pushed back farther in the paper as readers forget. There will be the social media posts: *Say her name, say her name, say her name.*

There will be the wing at the university named after you, butterflies pinned below panes of glass, *Lycaena Cupreus, Vanessa Cardui, Danaus plexippus,* wings splayed like stiff skirts. Your lover will attend the ceremony in your honor, drink from the plastic glasses of wine that are handed and handed to her, tap her knuckles against each windowed butterfly pane, *this place is a mausoleum.*

There will be spring rains and blossoming flowers and yards going yellow with dandelion dots, there will be the twist of wind pulling butterflies out your open door and into the brisk air of the spring world, into the cold of the world. They will spin and fall, spin and fall, and your lover will go back to your house for your things, sweep the rainbow of their broken wings into a dustpan and weep for the dying they have done with you.

She will spend a last night in your bed, inhale the scent of you from your pillowcase, will think *remember this, remember this.* She will stare open-eyed into the darkness and think how it is quieter than the flap of a butterfly wing in this place without you. She will think of the curl-wing butterfly tattoo on your left ankle, that she liked to trace the outline with her fingers, with her lips, said *what kind is this,* and you said, *it's nothing, it's just a dream,* and when she finally, briefly, sleeps, she will dream of you butterfly-winged, rising like smoke, wake with the word *wait* on her mouth, *wait* and *please*, hand outstretched, eyes tear-damp: *please, please wait.*

And in the morning, she will gather your things into the trunk of her car, grip the key copy in her hand, remember how you told her, like children do, *open your hand and close your eyes and you'll get a big surprise* before letting her curl her fingers around it. She'll put your favorite song on the car stereo, or the one she thinks of as *your song*, pull out into the street and be surrounded by the butterflies who hadn't died the day you did, suicide swirl of colorful wings dipping in and around the cars, and split-tailed swallows darting behind. She will reach for your hand that is no longer there, her hand will fall into the empty passenger seat, and she will say, *oh, it looks just like a dance.*

# Being the Murdered Whistleblower

The thing about being the murdered whistleblower is you set the plot in motion.

There will be federal agents in and out of the office building, arms heavy with boxes of paper, with computer hard drives, with video equipment. Your coworkers will stand beside their cars in the numbered parking lot, *but what will we do now, what will we do now?*

The vice president of the company will send an office-wide e-mail filled with vague and reassuring phrases, the vice president will have late-night dinners with expensive defense attorneys in silk ties, fresh-polished loafers.

He'll say: *They can get us for everything, can they? Not for* everything.

The vice president will have a smile that cracks, cracks, cracks.

Your coworkers will be interviewed one by one in the conference room upstairs, *I don't know anything, I never heard anything, this was just a paycheck for me.* The federal agents will make notes, will nod. Their ties will be polyester, their shoes cheap. Only one of them will remember your name.

She'll stop by your desk, look at the pinned-up photos of your gray-mix cat, printout *Onion* headlines, *Custodian taken into custody* will make her laugh, and one of the other agents will say *what is it?*

*Nothing,* she'll say. *It's nothing.*

She'll sit in on the interviews. She won't speak. The men will do the speaking, the men will lean in too close to your coworkers, the men will make sure their gun holsters show, the men will say *what do you remember, what do you know.*

They'll sit down with Helen from HR, Helen with her perfect bangs and roots just starting to show, Helen who volunteers with United Way, Helen who touched the back of your hand tenderly when you went to her about what had happened, who offered you a tissue from the box on her desk, *oh honey,* she said, *oh honey.* Helen who never filed your complaint, who ate lunch across the street that day with Amanda from Accounting, shook her head, *she just likes the attention, doesn't she.*

Helen from HR will jitter one foot while the federal agents interview her, left heel coming off the floor in fits, settling back down.

*I mean,* she'll say. *He's a good person.*

She'll say: *He'd never do those things like she said.*

The federal agents will nod, make notes in their pads.

Amanda from Accounting will be sitting in the break room with some of the other employees, the ones who aren't gossiping in the restroom, who aren't putting staplers, pens, notepads into their purses. Amanda from Accounting will be thinking about dyeing her hair a deeper shade of red, visiting Spain in the summer, Amanda from Accounting will practice saying, *Buenos dias, como estas, Buenos dias, como estas.*

*I'm not sad,* she'll say when the federal agents ask. *Why would I be sad?*

She'll say: *It's not like she was a good person.*

She'll say: *She just wanted to hurt him.*

The agents will nod, make notes.

*I mean,* Amanda from Accounting will say, tucking her hands into fists at her waist, *it's not like we were friends.*

Your other coworkers will agree, pockets littered with paper clips: *It's not like any of us were friends.*

Helen from HR will sit foot-jittering in the conference room. She will remember how fake it seemed when you began to cry in her office, how she saw you pinching the back of her hand to bring the tears to your eye, how she felt little bumps all over the back of your hand when she touched you, like you'd been pinching, pinching, pinching. The way you couldn't look her in the eye when you spoke, the way you couldn't show her proof, the way you didn't *have* any proof, the way you said *I'm so ashamed*, the way it sounded like a confession.

Helen from HR will face the federal agents, Helen from HR will have perfect posture.

She'll say again: *He's a good person.*

And the female agent will, finally, speak, while the men are taking their notes and nodding, while the men are adjusting their polyester ties.

*What makes you think,* she'll say, *he was a good man?*

Helen from HR will smile in a strained way, in a tight way, like she was only just waiting to be asked.

*He was never like that to me. He was always good to me.*

# Being the Murdered Dancer

The thing about being the murdered dancer is you set the plot in motion.

You will be found broken-backed, spotlight-lit on the stage. You will live long enough to whisper something to the stagehand who finds you, something that could be a plea, something that could be an accusation. He will notice the tearing of your tights, the way your mouth has gone blue-white, he will say *we'll get you some help, we'll get you some help,* he will try to understand what it is you said, that last wisp of breath before he leaned in close enough to hear.

The police will come for you with the coroner. The coroner will run the neighborhood funeral home, the coroner will see the bruising on your throat, the tearing of your fingernails.

He'll say: *It's a shame.*

He'll say: *It's a damn shame.*

The reporters will come after that, with notebook and pen in hand. You'll still be bent-doll on the stage, dead on the stage, and one will sneak a photo with his cell phone that gets put up on the paper's website before the decency complaints roll in.

The reporters will think you are too thin, the reporters will say *arms like toothpicks*. They will describe you using birds: *pigeon-toed, swan-necked, raven-haired*. They will say *beauty, fragile, broken*.

One reporter will remember the jewelry box that her parents gave her as a child, that she never stored jewelry in, but colorful paperclips instead, that she sometimes linked together and draped across her bedroom floor. She'll remember opening the jewelry box lid and a song playing when she did, a plastic dancer on a spring going jerkily round and round on one pointed little foot. She'll remember how it was magic to her, how it seemed just like magic.

She'll wonder if you had a jewelry box like that too, she'll wonder if you loved it the way she loved hers, opening and opening and opening it until something inside snapped and the little dancer drooped and bent and the song off-key played into silence.

*You're crying,* the night editor will tell her as she types up her article. *Did you know you're crying?*

You will be tumble-brought to the morgue, your body laid out on the cot in the back of the removal van. You will be put aside, put aside, and the show will go on.

The stage will come alight with dancers, the pit orchestra will play, briefly, *Somewhere Over the Rainbow* for head-bowed audience, the troupe director will dedicate the performance to you, your stand-in will collapse backstage at intermission in tears, the other dancers will crowd around her, dove-bobbing their worried heads, *do we need to stop, should we stop.*

*I'm fine,* she'll say, *I can do it, I'm fine,* bandage-wrap her bruised feet, come out for the second half as if nothing has happened, come out for the curtain call with the rest of the troupe, come out for the applause, the applause, the applause, and at the newspaper, the reporter will send her article to print and remember the sound of a broken jewelry box melody.

## Being the Murdered Waitress

The thing about being the murdered waitress is you set the plot in motion.

You will be found the next morning, when the prep cook comes in for his shift. Found like you had been lost. There will be crackle of glass across the floor, crunching under the soles of his work shoes. There will be slices of huckleberry pie and half-eaten grilled cheese sandwich. There will be a plate on the ground beside you, and the prep cook will stare at the plate instead of you, will bend to pick it up, as if picking it up will put everything back together.

When the busboy comes up behind him, he will startle in a way that implies guilt. The busboy will eye the prep cook suspiciously the rest of summer break, till he goes back to college, tells girls in bars, *I know a dead girl.*

The girls in bars will let him buy them whiskey sours, will think of him as *broken*, as *wounded*, will see something in the flicker of his eyes that they imagine is sorrow.

The busboy will take your story and make it his own. He'll tell the girls how hard you worked, how you never forgot an order, how you could balance three plates on one arm without needing a tray.

*She moved,* he'll say, *like a deer.*

He'll say: *Graceful, you know? But skittish.*

*Did you love her?* the girls will say, put their hands, on the bar, close to his. *It sounds like you loved her.*

The busboy will close his eyes, put his hand to his temple. He will do this every time they ask, first by accident, then by design.

*I did,* he'll say. *I think I did.*

The girls will sigh and shake their heads. They'll say: *How awful.*

The busboy won't go back to busing tables after that summer. The busboy will think *I'll never bus again*, take a part-time job making coffee in a drive-through kiosk, working slow evenings, pocketing coins from the leave-a-penny tray at the end of his shift, till he fills a jar with them. He'll heft the jar and the sound of their clatter will remind him of broken glass.

He'll think: *Now what? Now what?*

The prep cook won't leave the restaurant. The prep cook will start up the grill every morning, will remember how you'd come in after the lunch rush, put your hair up in the back room, tendrils of it slipping through your fingers, rubber band in your mouth. You watched your reflection in the window to the empty office, ghostly, warped, would call to the prep cook *did I get it all*, never wait for his answer.

The prep cook will flip pancakes and fry bacon for the morning regulars. They won't have known you, night-shift girl, but they'll ask. The morning waitress will pinch her lips, pour their coffee, *it's so sad, isn't it?*

The morning waitress will be offered night shifts, a bump in pay. The morning waitress will start carrying pepper spray. She'll smile, but not too much, at the night customers. She'll say, *oh, you kidders* when they ask for her number, when they call her, like they called you, *baby.* She'll keep one of the steak knives tucked in the pocket of her apron. She'll sit in her idling car in the parking lot before the shift starts, hands tense on the steering wheel. She'll breathe in for five counts, breathe out for twelve.

She'll think it's funny how much easier it is to let your breath go than to hold it. She'll say something about it to the prep cook when she comes in, *isn't it funny?* And he'll say *yes* and think of how his fingers bled when he plucked the shards of glass from his shoes, how each piece after that came out stained.

The former morning waitress will punch her timecard at the clock, tie her apron around her waist, feel for the weight of the steak knife in its pocket. Her hair will already be up, her hair will always already be up.

# Being the Murdered Hitchhiker

The thing about being the murdered hitchhiker is you set the plot in motion.

They'll remember seeing you by the side of the road, they'll remember your thumb out, *like in old television shows,* they'll think, they'll remember the ratty little suitcase at your feet.

*Not from around here,* they thought. Girls from *around here* know better than to hitchhike, than to wear skirts that short, than to sit on the curb at the end of the sidewalk, smoke, throw the butts into the gutter.

They'll remember they saw you before you were dead and they'll remember after, the flashing of police car lights, the orange cones coming out, the yellow tape going up. They'll remember the headlines, they'll remember *Mystery Girl,* they'll remember no one coming to claim you. They'll remember your body in the morgue for days, weeks, until the county finally promises you a burial in the transient cemetery, calls you *Jane Doe*.

Someone will put up a little white wooden cross where you are found, someone will leave flowers, someone will tie balloons to a brick and set them there, and one will float away, soft pink one, into the sky, and people will look up, say, *there it goes, oh, there it goes.*

They will wonder what kind of girl you were before. They'll picture you like their own daughters, bedroom doors closed, slips of light peeking out from underneath, sitting home on Saturday nights, singing along to Patty Loveless. They'll picture you like their black sheep cousins calling home on Christmas eve, *hey, could you send some money, I ran into some trouble, I just need a few bucks.* They'll picture you like Louise Brooks in that silent movie they saw bits and pieces of flipping through the channels on a bored Sunday afternoon, *on the lam,* they'll think, *in disguise,* they'll think.

They'll put little things down around your cross shrine, they won't think about the spill of your blood there, the blanking of your eyes, the hitching of your last breaths. They'll lay down teddy bears, unlit lavender candles, flowers plucked from front-yard gardens. They'll leave things for you when no one else is looking, and when the schoolchildren walk past the place you were found, crossing their fingers and squeezing closed their eyes, they'll say *elves*, like in the fairy tale with the cobbler, they'll say *elves did it.*

Your shrine will grow and grow. No one will take anything from it, no one will touch. It will spill over sidewalk edge; the schoolchildren will cross on the other side, the schoolchildren will say *did you know this place is haunted.* They will pile up pebbles on the opposite side of the street. They will think of *evening out*, they will think of *balance.*

And when the winter comes, the snow will bury it all, shrine and pebble pile, and your ragged suitcase where it had been thrown blocks and blocks away, and it won't be until spring that it all comes bare and uncovered, and you are remembered once again.

# Being the Murdered Detective

The thing about being the murdered detective is you set the plot in motion.

Your partner will *go rogue.* He'll go on the hunt for your killer, track down former suspects, grab them by the collar. He'll *rough them up,* scrape and scar his knuckles, wipe away blood on the back of his dark slacks, say: *Was it you? Was it you?*

Your partner will take *unnecessary risks.* Your partner will become a *loose cannon.*

Your partner will eat whisper-dry meals with his cow-eyed wife under flickering kitchen light. The shadows will dance around them. Their eldest son will be quietly failing college, drinking cheap beer stowed under his dorm bed at night. Their youngest will lock himself in his bedroom, play video games in the dark. Your partner and his wife will flinch at the sound of simulated gunfire through his door.

*Did you love her,* your partner's wife will say. She will have her meatloaf cut into crumble bits on her plate before her; she won't be able to look at him. She will have never liked you, the way you carried a holstered gun, the way you wore your top two blouse buttons undone, the way you were the name in her husband's mouth from morning to night. Her upper lip will twitch, *did you love her.*

*She was my partner.*

*But did you* love *her,* smack her hands down on the table on either side of her plate, rattle the silverware, spill her wine.

Your partner won't answer, push his plate away, rise from the table, *I can't talk to you when you're like this,* leave his wife there, flicker of shadow spanning her face.

Your partner will be haunted by the ghost of you, caught in glimpses on reflective surfaces, flat of toaster in the morning, frost scrapes on car windshield, sun glare on dark glasses. He'll see the turning of your head in reflection, curl of your hair, tilt of your chin, he'll say your name, say your name, say your name.

He'll drink coffee at night, cheap scotch in the middle of the day, drink in throat-searing slugs that warm him from the pit of his belly, that hollow him whole. He'll forget to shave for days, look at his bearded image in the shower-fogged mirror, trace your name in the condensation, say *I'll find him, I will.*

His wife will pack a bag, take the youngest son with her to her sister's in the suburbs, his wife will say *call when you're ready to be the man you used to be again*, his wife will say, *we'll be waiting.*

Your partner will bring your old case files home in banker's boxes. He'll stack them in the kitchen, read them under the light that dims and dims, eat three-day-old rice seasoned with ketchup, write down suspect names in a notepad, cross them out. He'll hear a sound from the other room, or think he does, draw his weapon, cock the hammer. He'll contemplate the pistol in his hands, he'll think *if only, if only.*

He'll *go too far.* There will be complaints, lawsuits, disciplinary action. He'll lose his badge, he'll lay it down on the sergeant's desk beside his gun, he'll unloosen his tie, unbutton the cuffs of his shirt. He'll be told to get himself together, he'll be told *get your head on straight*, he'll laugh, laugh, bitter laugh.

He'll go to the neighborhood cop bar. He'll drink, he'll drink, he'll stumble and slur, get taken home by a sympathetic colleague, *if it was my partner, I don't know* what *I'd do.* He'll wake to aching head, flickering kitchen light, he'll think *tomorrow I will fix it, tomorrow I will.*

His wife will come to check on him in the morning, his wife will find him on the ground beside shattered light bulb, will kneel beside him, put her arms around his shoulders, think *they feel thinner than they used to,* think *he is fading away.*

*It's going to be all right, it's going to be all right now,* she'll say, and, holding him, she will see a reflection in the broken glass on the kitchen floor, something both dark and light, something shining, something that could be you, something that could be nothing at all.

# Being the Murdered Indian

The thing about being the murdered Indian is you set the plot in motion.

You will be sunbleached bones and fabric strips, snag of hair on root-exposed tree. You will be page 12 news, you will be the feds telling your parents *girls run away, it happens, she's probably fine.*

They will say *girls like you.* They will say and they will say *girls like you.*

You will be photos on posters at the rez grocery store, you will be *I miss yous* on your friends' Facebook pages, the box of your favorite things in your parents' trailer. You will be the empty look in your mother's eyes when she dials the feds, when the line rings and rings, when she holds, holds, holds, when she says *is there any news* and they say *no,* say, *no, check back in six months.*

You will be your older sister taking in your kids, you will be the name they have forgotten. You will be the way your sister winces when the littlest calls her *mama*, the way she says *no, no, you have a mama and she's coming back.*

The way she says: *She's coming back.*

You will be the birthday cake your mother makes every year, the way she increases the candles by one, the way she clutches the fabric of her skirt every Sunday at church when the pastor says *have hope.*

*Have hope.*

You will be the sunny days that your children go out to play, the way they run up and down the street till the neighbor's pickup comes by, till he says *you kids, don't play in the road, you'll get yourselves killed,* and they'll dart away from his idling truck, laughing, laughing, and he will think that you used to laugh like that too.

You will be the unworn moccasins in the bottom of the box at your parents' place, you will be the way your mother pulls them out from time to time, checks for loose beads, runs her thumb over the circular design, says, *my little one,* the way she says *oh, my little one.*

You will be the way your father dies never knowing, the way your family leaves a space in the chapel where you would have sat, the way your uncle keens and beats his fist against his chest, after, in the parking lot, glaring up at the cloud-wisp sky, the ghost-milk moon hanging there.

You will be the *this number has been disconnected* recording, you will be the apologetic secretary your mother finally reaches: *We thought someone had told you, someone should have told you the number changed,* you will be the way the secretary taps the desk with the end of her pen, *tip-tip-tip-tip-tap,* the way she says: *there's no news,* hangs up the phone, sighs.

You will be the way your oldest daughter can't sleep through the night, the way she sits rigid-backed in school, the way she gets perfect scores in math, the way she is accused of cheating by her teachers, crying into your sister's lap later *can't I just be smart, can't I be that,* the way she will start going with boys in cracked-windshield cars, drink beer with them on the hood. The way she will let them kiss her, the way she will lean back and close her eyes, the way she will sometimes remember how it felt to hold your hand.

You will be the quiet of the highway before a semi rumbles through, you will be the pavement cracked with dandelion sprout. You will be the window at your sister's place that never quite closes, the whistle-hiss of wind at night.

You will be twenty years gone, you will be the hiker stumbling on loose dirt, you will be the bleach of white in the foliage, you will be gone, you will be gone, you will be gone.

# ACKNOWLEDGEMENTS

Thank you to all of my writer friends who have always supported me – Pat, Audra, Ashley, Kristen, Melissa, Lori, Chloe, and Noa especially – but to all of my writer friends who have offered kind words and encouragement. It means so much to me.

Thank you to Sarah for her beautiful art.

Thank you to Eric, Genevieve, and all of the journal editors who published my work for believing in me and in these stories. I am so, so grateful.

And thank you, most of all, to my daughter Persephone, who listens and reads and cares. I wish strength and courage and beauty for her in all her life.


"Being the Murdered Girl" first appeared in *Crab Fat Magazine*.

"Being the Murdered Wife" first appeared in *Bad Pony Magazine*.

"Being the Murdered Lover" first appeared in *Cotton Xenomorph*.

"Being the Murdered Actress" first appeared in *Cleaver Magazine*.

"Being the Murdered Coed" first appeared in *Pithead Chapel.*

"Being the Murdered Babysitter" first appeared in *Passages North.*

"Being the Murdered Homecoming Queen" first appeared in *Wyvern Lit.*

"Being the Murdered Clerk" first appeared in *Gravel Magazine.*

"Being the Murdered Teacher" first appeared in *Mojave River.*

"Being the Murdered Bride" first appeared in *Gigantic Sequins.*

"Being the Murdered Moll" first appeared in *Cheap Pop.*

"Being the Murdered Professor" first appeared in *Fictive Dream.*

"Being the Murdered Student" first appeared in *Moria.*

"Being the Murdered Mother" first appeared in *Rhythm Bones Lit.*

"Being the Murdered Extra" first appeared in *Craft.*

"Being the Murdered Mermaid" first appeared in *Gordon Square Review.*

"Being the Murdered Mama" first appeared in *Puerto Del Sol.*

"Being the Murdered Chanteuse" first appeared in *Orange Blossom Review.*

# ABOUT THE AUTHOR

Cathy Ulrich is the founding editor of *Milk Candy Review*, a journal of flash fiction. Her work has been published in various journals, including *Black Warrior Review, Passages North,* and *Wigleaf* and can be found in *Best Microfiction* 2019, *Best Small Fictions* 2019, and Wigleaf's Top 50 Very Short Fictions 2017 and 2019. She lives in Montana with her daughter and various small animals.

Made in the USA
Monee, IL
06 March 2020